The European Economic Community and Mexico

Euro-Latin American Relations – The Omagua Series

General Editor:

Peter Coffey, Europa Institute, University of Amsterdam

The Omagua were a civilised and peaceful Indian tribe living in the Amazon region, between present-day Peru, Ecuador and Brazil, in the fifteenth and sixteenth centuries.

The European Economic Community and Mexico

Edited by

PETER COFFEY and MIGUEL S. WIONCZEK

1987

Martinus Nijhoff Publishers

A MEMBER OF THE KLUWER ACADEMIC PUBLISHERS GROUP

DORDRECHT / BOSTON / LANCASTER

IV

Distributors

for the United States and Canada: Kluwer Academic Publishers, P.O. Box 358, Accord Station, Hingham, MA 02018-0358, USA
for the UK and Ireland: Kluwer Academic Publishers, MTP Press Limited, Falcon House, Queen Square, Lancaster LA1 1RN, UK
for all other countries: Kluwer Academic Publishers Group, Distribution Center, P.O. Box 322, 3300 AH Dordrecht, The Netherlands

Library of Congress Cataloging in Publication Data

```
The European Economic Community and Mexico.

    (Euro-Latin American relations - the Omagua series)
    Includes index.
    1. European Economic Community--Mexico.  2. European
Economic Community countries--Foreign economic
relations--Mexico.  3. Mexico--Foreign economic
relations--European Economic Community countries.
I. Coffey, Peter.  II. Wionczek, M. S. (Miguel S.)
III. Series.
HC241.25.M6E97   1986      341.24'22       86-5355
ISBN 90-247-3326-X
```

ISBN 90-247-3326-X (this volume)
ISBN 90-247-3325-1 (series)

PRINTED IN THE NETHERLANDS

Foreword

The relationship between Europe and Latin America has in the years following the Second World War gone from one of distance and apathy to growing mutual interest and importance. In a world where two super-powers appear to have established themselves as arbiters of the fate of mankind the role of Europe, a potential battleground between them, is a difficult one. For their part Latin Americans living in the shadow of one super-power and threatened with involvement in East-West tension in the Caribbean Basin have an equally difficult problem to face.

The establishment of the Institute for European-Latin American Relations (IRELA) on the initiative of a group of Europeans and Latin Americans is one manifestation of the desire of both regions to come closer together. Within its limited resources it is seeking to promote study of the bilateral relationship and make that relationship more meaningful, not only in academia, but also in the world of politics and culture.

The European-Latin American enterprise represented by this new series of studies and inaugurated by this volume dedicated to the European Community and Mexico is a testimony to the desire of the two regions to know each other better and strengthen their relations. Involved as I am in the workings of our new Institute, I am sure this book will serve as a model for many other studies to come.

HUGH O'SHAUGHNESSY

Preface

After more than two decades of relative neglect by the European Economic Community of countries in Latin America, the year 1985 - when under the aegis of the European Parliament, the Institute for Relations between Europe and Latin America (IRELA) was installed in Madrid - seemed to mark a turning point in relations between the two sides. This event - together with the return to democracy by a number of Latin American countries and the unrelated economic and debt problems experienced by these countries - has created a most auspicious moment for the launch of a new multi-disciplinary series of books on Europe and Latin America.

Although there exists a considerable amount of bi-lateral academic collaboration between academics on both sides of the Atlantic, and despite a growing degree of co-operation between European Community institutions and sub-regional Latin American groupings - such as the Andean Pact and the Central American Common Market - knowledge about the European Community and Latin America tends to be restricted to groups of experts. It is therefore desirable that this awareness and knowledge be disseminated among a wider audience. Consequently, it is the hope of the editors that this book will constitute a substantial first move in this direction.

It is fitting that the first work in this series should be the product of collaboration between the Europa Instituut of the University of Amsterdam and the Colegio de Mexico, in Mexico City. Both institutes have, for many years, undertaken research both at national and international levels and have adopted a conscious policy of deepening their international scientific relations.

The editors are pleased with the response by their colleagues in different countries who have agreed to make contributions to this book.

VIII

They are also grateful to the Dutch publishing company, Martinus Nijhoff, which, in the persons of Alexander Schimmelpenninck and Alan Stephens, has encouraged research in the field of European and Latin American Relations and has agreed to publish this new series of books.

PETER COFFEY and MIGUEL WIONCZEK
Amsterdam and Mexico City
December 1985

Contents

Notes about the Contributors

Hugh O'Shaughnessy is the Vice-President of the Executive Committee of the Institute for European-Latin American Relations. He is the Latin American Correspondent of *The Observer*.

Alfonso Cebreros is the Coordinator of the Mexican National Food Commission.

Peter Coffey, a British national, is Head of the Economics Section at the Europa Instituut, University of Amsterdam. He is also the general international editor of this new series of books on Europe and Latin America.

Elisabeth de Ghellinck, a Belgian national, is an assistant professor at the Centre de Recherches Interdisciplinaires Droit et Economie Industrielle (CRIDE) at the Catholic University of Louvain. She is also an associate professor of economics at the Catholic University of Mons, Belgium.

Fernando de Mateo, is chief adviser at the Mexican Foreign Trade Institute.

Jorge Eduardo Navarrete, is the Mexican Ambassador in the United Kingdom and a former undersecretary for economic affairs at the Mexican Foreign Ministry.

Piet van den Noort, a Dutch national, is a professor of economics at the Wageningen Agricultural University in the Netherlands.

XII

Heinz Gert Preusse, a German national, is Head of the Foreign Trade and Development Division at the Ibero-Amerika Institut für Wirtschaftsforschung, Göttingen University, West Germany.

Alfred Tovias, a Spanish national, is a senior lecturer in the Department of International Relations at the Hebrew University, Jerusalem, Israel.

Saúl Trejo Reyes, is a senior research fellow at El Colegio de Mexico. He was economic adviser to the President (1976-1982) and is a former director of the National Minimum Wages Commision.

Miguel S. Wionczek, is the director of the Energy Research Programme at El Colegio de Mexico and is a former deputy director general of the National Council for Science and Technology.

Acknowledgements

The editors are most grateful to the translators at the Colegio de Mexico who have given great satisfaction in translating the Spanish language contributions into English. Thanks are also due to Howard Gold, a librarian at the Europe Instituut, who has prepared the index for this book. Similarly, the editors wish to thank Mr. Ben Kotmans, a secretary at the Europa Instituut, who has typed the index and certain parts of this book. The secretaries at the Colegio de Mexico are also thanked for typing the contributions written by our Mexican colleagues.

PART 1
COOPERATION, TRADE AND INVESTMENT

Mexico and the European Economic Community: Trade and Investment

FERNANDO DE MATEO

I Introduction

Over the last few years, the whole process of structural change in developing countries has begun to evolve very rapidly. The economies of these countries have grown at a faster rate in the services and technology sectors than in the more traditional industrial fields and in fact most of the jobs created during the last ten years have been in these fast-growing sectors. This situation has had a considerable impact on both developing and industrialized countries.

Industrialized countries have had to face a series of problems in their transition towards post-industrialization. The changes occurring in the type of employment and productive capacity required has met with heavy resistance from the workers or businessmen affected. Thus, a paradoxical situation has arisen whereby there is unemployment *and* there are also jobs available but they cannot be filled for lack of qualified workers.

Also characteristic of this transition are the attempts of those affected to maintain their status quo through protectionist measures, often with the active approval of their respective governments. The authorities responsible for trade policy are sometimes undecided as to the convenience of imposing import restrictions and it is not uncommon to find that the Executive of a given country objects to the application of this sort of measure whilst the government's Legislative Power condones it. Generally speaking, certain committments are made that do not always coincide with the interests of free trade.

The negative impact these neo-protectionist measures designed to increase export earnings have on developing countries is clear. What is less obvious is the effect the industrialized countries' transition towards a post-industrial stage will have on these same export earnings. As the demand for raw materials for industrial production decreases, a world market glut will be created for many of those products exported by the developing countries, which will obviously have a direct effect on prices. This, together with the developing countries' slow rate of growth during the last ten years and the overvalued US dollar (almost all raw materials are priced in US dollars), has caused raw materials prices to drop to their lowest level since the Korean War.

Consequently, developing countries' export earnings are being undermined on two counts. On the one hand, neo-protectionism is affecting their non-traditional exports, while on the other, the low prices of their raw material exports has reduced their importing capacity even further, which is in turn under considerable pressure with the debt servicing obligations arising from countries' enormous foreign debt.

The transformation process from an industrial society to a post-industrial one is not exclusive of the United States. The European Economic Community countries have in fact been immersed in this process for a number of years, even though they are somewhat behind in certain advanced technological fields as compared to the United States and Japan.

There has been a noticeable drop in the growth rate of the European countries since 1973 attributable to three main causes[1]:
1) a long-term reduction in Europe's increased productivity as it reached similar levels to the United States;
2) unavoidable cyclical losses in production and in jobs as these countries adjusted to major shocks to the system;
3) losses due to changes occurring in institutional views on macropolitical measures.

As regards the first point, European countries enjoyed a very high rate of growth all through the fifties and sixties as they were able to take advantage of the concessions given to "backward" nations. It was inevitable that these abnormally high levels of production would gradually subside as they caught up with the United States. The above-mentioned shocks to the system have had an adverse effect on economic activity since the early seventies, as was the case with the collapse of the Bretton Woods monetary system and the twelve-fold increase in oil prices. The magnitude of these shocks was such that they brought about changes in macroeconomic policy as well as in the rules of the game played by those responsible for public finances. Furthermore, changes even occured in the expectations of the private sector. Lastly, the fall in the Community's economic growth was also due to the deliberate caution adopted in the application of policy.[2] Thus, as a result of insufficient economic growth in the European Economic Community and in the industrialized countries in general, the growth prospects of the developing countries have been affected because of the foreign trade multipliers.

Deindustrialization has accelerated in almost all of the EEC countries, particularly France, West Germany and the Netherlands and is a consequence of recent events as well as the long-term factors previously mentioned. There is less elasticity in the demand for industrial products than there was during the first few years after World War II. Growth in productivity in this sector is rapid and competition from recently industrialized developing countries has increased. Moreover, there has been a recent reduction in the demand for industrial products, especially capital goods and other intermediate inputs. On the other hand, the services sector shows greater cyclical sensitivity and greater long-term elasticity of demand and growth in productivity than does industry.

Needless to say, the European economy tends to show much greater foreign aperture. In fact, in every case the ratio of merchandise exported to GNP has grown steadily since the end of the Second World War, being higher than that recorded in 1929. It is interesting to note that the EEC countries' economies are much more open to foreign trade than are the United States and Japan, as can be seen in Table 1.

After ten years of an economic growth rate lower than the EEC's real potential, prices are growing at a similar rate as in the sixties, although the amount of unused capacity in skilled labour as well as physical capital is very high. Also, the economic policy followed by the Community is extremely cautious and those countries that tried to grow inde-

Table 1. Merchandise exports to GNP ratio

	1929	1938	1950	1960	1973	1982
Germany	15.3	5.6	8.5	15.7	19.4	26.7
United States	5.0	3.6	3.6	4.0	5.3	6.9
France	14.0	6.0	10.6	11.2	14.3	17.0
Japan	16.0	14.9	7.8	9.4	9.0	13.0
Netherlands	29.4	18.4	28.6	36.1	39.8	48.3
United Kingdom	15.5	8.4	16.7	15.9	17.1	20.5

Source: A. Maddison, *op.cit.*, p.600

pendently of the international trend were eventually obliged to conform, as was the case of Germany in 1979 and France in 1981. This corroborates more and more the tendency towards international economic interdependence that has been created over the last four decades, despite the existence of a fluctuating monetary exchange system which theoretically should allow each country to apply its economic policy independently.[3]

II The EEC's Industrial Policy

Within this general context, the transition from an industrial society to a post-industrial one could take place through state intervention or in responce to market forces. The latter is based on the use of economic policy measures designed to promote a decentralized system of competition wherein industrial adjustment is automatic and continuous. In other words, industrial policy is in this case a series of measures aimed at promoting vigorous and efficient competition.

The interventionist industrial policy also takes into account the measures utilized by the different governments or general authorities, like the EEC Commision, in order to include industrial development in an overall economic program aimed at achieving sectorial, national and regional objectives. Of course the degree of interventionism resorted to may vary depending on the country involved, and the measures utilized may also differ considerably amongst themselves. The choice between an industrial policy based on market forces and one on intervention depends on the state's political and economic stance, together with the government's confidence, or lack of it, in its own competitiveness as a means to achieve objectives such as technical progress, higher living standards, fair distribution of income, etc.

> The differences between the two types of policy appear to a certain point to be theoretical, particularly in the case of mixed economies like the European. There is a continuity in the degree of interventionism employed here. In some European countries there are sectors affected by public macro-economic measures aimed at introducing or promoting the structural change, while others remain untouched by the rules governing the market. In the same token, if one considers countries such as Germany and France, their industrial policies are very different officially, the one being subject to market conditions and the other being interventionist. In actual fact, they are very similar, particularly if the differences between their respective industrial structures are considered.[4]

According to Ghellinck, the industrial policy implicit in the Treaty of Rome is one based on domestic competition and the creation of a common competitive market. Once domestic tariffs are abolished, the measures introduced are designed to guarantee this common market, that is to say, a competitive policy, a common foreign policy and the power to harmonize the laws of the member states.

During the fifties and sixties, the countries of the Community underwent extremely high growth rates which in fact made it easier to establish the EEC itself. However, during the seventies, these countries' economies faced a substantial reduction in their economic growth, an increase in the level of unemployment, growing competition from developing countries in the European countries' traditional exports, such as textiles, steel and ship building, as well as increasing competition from the United States and Japan in high-tech industries.

This created growing scepticism in the industrial policy's approach to the market and placed more pressure on the Community to protect its industry by establishing tariff and non-tariff barriers, aid programs, internal regulations governing technical standards, etc.

To cope with this situation, the Commission took action in the two following ways. First, it used things like competition and trade policy at its disposal to achieve industrial policy objectives. Secondly, it took up the role of policy innovator by introducing several proposals advocating more positive action in Europe's industrial policy.[5]

However, despite the Commission's desire to undertake positive action, up until now the Member States have not granted it the power to do so - the Community's industrial policy continues to be based on competition and essentially negative action. Where structural problems exist in industries throughout the Community, as in ship building, textiles, artificial fibres, steel, etc., specific outlines have been formulated to aid the enterprises affected. However, the dominant factor in this process of adjustment lies in the bilateral agreements drawn up between the Community and other countries with the aim of giving external protection to these industries, but where the comparative advantage has been passed on to certain developing countries.

As labour costs become the most important factor in an industry's competitiveness, it is quite possible that Community protectionist measures could be extended to a growing number of industries. The reason for this is that the specific policies proposed by the Commission dealing with structural adjustment contain mainly palliative measures to protect the Community's production as it gradually loses its competitiveness, instead of efficient measures designed to allow an orderly transferral of these productive processes towards developing countries.[6]

III Common Agricultural Policy

Common agricultural policy has always been a fundamental component of the European Economic Community and the subject of a very large number of books, articles and documents. This paper will only deal with its outstanding characteristics, particularly those related to the protectionist measures taken in this area.

There is a long tradition of protection given to farming in Europe stemming both from an attempt to attain self-sufficiency in farming production and reduce its dependence on international suppliers in emergency situations, and also from the desire to provide farmers with an income similar to that received by the other sectors of the economy. By doing so, the Community has actually managed to restrain the farming population's exodus to the industrial and services sectors. The common agricultural policy is the centre of the community economic policy and it has been said that if it were to be dismantled, the EEC would disappear.

Although the Common Agricultural Policy depends largely on restraint, one could say that it coincides with the GATT's guidelines in that it can apply quantitive restrictions when domestic production of a given product is controlled or when there is a production surplus. Not only has the Common Agricultural Policy (CAP) transformed the Community into the world's biggest producer of certain goods it had previously had to import, but it has also converted it into a major exporter of many of these same products. It is now the world's biggest exporter of milk products and is second in meat and sugar. As a result, it has been accused of causing a world wide fall in the price of foodstuffs.

The CAP's objectives are as follows:

> a) to increase agricultural productivity through technical development, rational development of agricultural production and optimum utilization of those factors related to production, particularly labour; b) to assure a good standard of living for the farming population...; c) to establish markets; d) to guarantee regular supply; and e) to assure reasonable prices to the consumer.[7]

For this purpose, in 1968 the harmonization of agricultural markets was established. Currently this market is governed by 21 basic regulations dealing with different branches of agricultural production, such as seedlings, cut flowers, and ornamental shrubs, certain products shown in Annex 2 of the Treaty of Rome, raw tobacco, linen and hemp, hops, fruit and vegetables, dry forage, fish and seafood, wine, processed fruit and vegetable products, seeds oils and fats, lamb and goats meat, cereals, rice, pork, eggs, poultry, beef, milk and milk products.

The system also includes four additional regulations concerning trade agreements involving products not subject to the rules of the common agricultural market and derived from the processing of agricultural products or those that may be used to substitute the same. The common organization of agricultural markets involves price control, subsidies on the production and commercialization of several products, storage facilities and a common administrative system for stabilizing both imports and exports.

Apart from these internal measures, a common trading system is applied at the Community's border on the following products: sugar, processed fruit and vegetable products, pork, eggs, poultry, rice, beef and milk products. This trading system works in such a way that when the world price of a given product falls below the EEC price, a tax is charged on all imports of this product equal to the difference between the threshold price set annually and the cif price calculated according to the lowest international market price. This mechanism is known as variable levies.

In order to keep track of trading transactions with outsiders and to determine the resulting trends, all imports and exports in the most important farming sectors must be done with the corresponding import or export license. However, the variable levies system is so efficient that only under very unusual circumstances is it necessary to resort to quantitative restrictions. One such occasion arose in July 1974 and March 1977 when beef imports were suspended.

Table 2. Tariff equivalents to the variable levies on selected products

	Butter	Oleaginous seeds	Wheat	Corn	Sugar	Meat	Rice
1975/76	220	27	24	28	9	96	37
1976/77	301	21	104	63	76	92	66
1977/78	288	53	116	103	155	96	28
1978/79	303	61	93	101	176	99	57
1979/80	411	85	63	90	90	104	31

Source: A. Cairncross, *et al*,"Protectionism: Threat to International Order - The Impact on Developing Countries", The Commonwealth Secretariat, London, 1982. Quoted in Sieglinde Reichenbach, "Protectionism in the EEC and its implications to developing countries". UNIDO, July 11, 1984.

The level of protection given by the variable levies has been calculated by the different authorities according to their *ad valorem* equivalents. For example, the calculation of certain agricultural products' *ad valorum* equivalence done by Alec Cairncross *et al* are shown in Table 2.

The protection afforded by these variable levies is theoretically infinite if one considers that if the exporters lower their prices, all that happens is that more income is received from the taxes imposed on the goods imported into the Community. This trading system in fact isolates the producers and consumers of agricultural products from the impact of the fluctuation of supply and demand on the world market. This isolation combined with guaranteed prices to the farmer has brought about an increase in agricultural productivity within the EEC of 6.7 percent per annum between 1968-1973 and 2.5 percent between 1973 and 1980.[8]

Community consumption of agricultural products showed a much slower increase however, which created large surpluses in different sectors at different times. In order to get rid of this excess production the Community subsidized exports, thus directly affecting many of the exporting developing countries, especially Latin America. On the one hand, the access of these latter countries to the Community market is extremely restricted by the CAP's external measures. On the other hand, the Community's subsidized exports compete with the exports of these countries on outside markets, which reduces their export capacity even further.

IV Relations with Latin America

The European Economic Community's per capita income is almost US $ 7000 per annum, it has 272 million inhabitants, it produces 20 percent of the world's gross national product, it has 31 percent of the world's monetary reserves and 35 percent of its trade and its GNP amounts to around two trillion dollars. Latin America's income per capita is US $ 1500, it has 370 million inhabitants, it produces 5.5 percent of the world gross national product, it participates in 4 percent of world trade and its GNP amounts to 550 billion dollars.

These figures show the vast difference in the development of both regions. Furthermore, having grown at an average annual rate of 6 percent for two decades, Latin America's economy had negative growth during 1981, 1982 and 1983, and grew only slightly in 1984. Its per capita income has fallen almost 10 percent since 1980. Its foreign debt amounts to 370,000 million dollars and interest payments reach 40,000 million dollars per annum, which absorbs more than 35 percent of its total export earnings. Since 1980, the rate at which the region's productive capital is utlized fell 13 percent and debt servicing in some countries absorbs up to 25 percent of their GNP. In brief, Latin America's economy is undergoing its worst recession since the time of the Great Depression.

The recovery of the Latin American economy as a whole will depend essentially on two factors. The first is the sustained recovery of the industrial countries' economy, leading in turn to growth and liberalization of international trade. The second factor is a change in the direction of the flow of foreign investment towards Latin America.

As a whole, Europe provides 26 percent of all Latin America's imports and receives 28 percent of its exports. Europe's direct and indirect investments in Latin America maintained sustained growth during the last few decades before the current economic recession. It should therefore be of particular interest to Europe that Latin America find a favorable solution to its economic and financial problems.

On the one hand, it is in the interests of the EEC that Latin American exports recover their former vitality. But this could only happen if the EEC were to loosen up its import restrictions and create more favorable conditions for Latin America's exports, particularly manufactured goods and commodities of interest to the subcontinent. It should also look for ways to make its products more attractive to Latin American markets and increase financing of its exports, particularly capital goods, to Latin America. Furthermore, the Community should try to encourage the flow of direct investment towards Latin America with the aim of revitalizing trade between the two regions.

Equally as important as a continuous flow of capital towards Latin America is a massive and institutionalized supply of technology. However, the European Economic Community Commission gives very little priority to its foreign relations, giving preference to the 65 ACP countries, then the Mediterranean countries and lastly those of the Western Pacific and South East Asia.

Considering the Community's economic situation and the low priority given to Latin American relations, it is not surprising that the CE-GRULA dialogue was a virtual failure. After a recess of two years owing to the Falkland Islands upheaval, the European Economic Community drew up a document designed to strengthen relations between Latin America and the Community.[9]

In this document the Community acknowledge that Latin American exports to the European Economic Community have dropped relatively speaking during the last few years. Latin America's share in the Community's imports fell from 11 percent in 1958 to 5.5 percent in 1982. This reduction was caused by the preferential relations between the Community and the ACP countries, the Mediterranean countries and members of the EFTA, together with the Common Agricultural Policy and the restrictions placed on a number of industrial products in which some Latin American countries have a comparative advantage. The document also admits that the help given to these developing countries in particular has been insufficient. Nevertheless, it is pointed out that as far as trading policy is concerned, "the margin available for consolidated action on the part of the Community is extremely small, at least in the short and medium-term".[10]

As regards a possible transference of resources, the document mentions that "the Communities' institutions are not in a position to assume an active role in improving or helping to solve Latin America's debt payment problems". However, the Commission is of the opinion that the European Investment Bank should be invited to use its financing capacity outside the Community in Latin America and that the projects financed by the bank should be of mutual interest and be studied on the basis of traditional criteria and rules. Special attention should be given to the possibility of joint financing and the Community should be willing to cooperate actively in organizing and encouraging financial consortiums. To date no definite progress has been made in this field.

The EEC's reduced growth, resistence to an orderly and efficient restructuring of international industry, the high rate of unemployment in the Community countries, a reluctance to modify the CAP, the problems involved in organizing Spain and Portugal's entry into the Community and the low priority given to Latin America have all reduced the above-mentioned dialogue to a mere exercise in diplomacy with more political than economic value.

V Protection to Industry[11]

The weighted average of the external common tariff for industrial products is 2.9 percent, whereas for the United States it is 4.3 percent and for Japan, 7 percent. This figure is only a very rough estimate as the variation in the exchange rates for the major trading countries during one week alone can result in a higher figure. Thus, at first glance it would appear that the Community's protective tariff system is practically non-existent. However, the afore-mentioned figure is only an average and does not reflect the very high protective tariffs placed on certain products of particular interest to developing countries. For example, the nominal tariff for honey is 27 percent, for bananas it is 20 percent, some vegetable fats have up to 10 percent tax, cocoa pays 15 percent and coffee essences and concentrates 18 percent. To these must be added the domestic discriminatory taxes applied to some of these products by certain Community countries.

The tariff reductions made to products such as textiles, clothing, shoes and leather goods during the Tokyo Round were very small. In fact, the protection afforded to these and other products of interest to Latin America can sometimes reach more than 60 percent. This excessive protection is highly discriminatory if one considers the preferential agreements entered into by the European Economic Community and the countries of the EFTA, the Mediterranean, i.e. Morocco, Algeria, Malta, Cyprus, Egypt, Israel, Jordan, Lebanon, Syria and Yugoslavia, and the ACP. These agreements exclude most non-agricultural products from these countries from tariffs within the EEC apart from giving certain advantages to several agricultural products.

For the rest of the developing nations, this generalized preferential system reduces somewhat the effect of the tariffs in the most favored nation (MFN) arrangement. This preferential treatment is applied to 140 countries and territories and was extended to Rumania in 1974 and the Chinese People's Republic in 1980. The Community scheme covers all manufactured and semi-manufactured products and around 300 agricultural products not subject to variable levies. The preferential treatment given to industrial products consists of total exemption from these tariffs. The levies are either partially or totally reduced for agricultural products.

However, most of the exportable industrial products from Latin American countries with tax-free access to the Common Market are still controlled by quotas or a maximum limit. In general these quotas are set as a maximum quantity, mainly in the case of textiles and clothing, or a maximum value. As soon as the allowed maximum is reached, imports at preferential rates are suspended immediately and all subsequent imports have to pay MFN rates.

Statistical data is kept on other products receiving preferential treatment and which are not subject to quotas. When certain imports threaten to cause economic problems to any of the EEC countries, a levy is imposed on the product in question so as to limit is importation.

Over the years, the Community's preferential scheme has become more restrictive. In the case of one particular country, for example, its share in one given product went from 50 percent to 30 percent, and then from 20 percent to 15 percent. The growth rate in the allowed global quota for each product has also fallen considerably to 5 percent or even 0 percent where the product is considered to be "sensitive".

However, the quantitive restrictions scheme has become somewhat more transparent after preferences were modified in 1981. From then on, quotas were fixed only for those sensitive products from developing countries considered to be competitive. Most of the maximum limits were abolished and most of the remaining restrictions became specific, as in the case of imports from particular countries, as opposed to global. This has implied considerable discrimination between the different beneficiary countries. But in that same year, new restrictions were imposed on imports from the more advanced developing countries, like Mexico.[12] In a large number of products the maximum limit for preferential imports has not been raised since 1982.

The granting of preferences on textiles and clothing by the EEC is linked to the Multi-fibre Arrangement signed in the GATT whereby these preferences are given to those countries that have agreed to restrict exports "voluntarily". Furthermore, maximum quotas are established before these products can enter into the preferential regime. Each country's share of the quota is based on its competitive power and its level of development. All in all, the scheme is extremely restrictive for these products.

It should be pointed out that the General System of Preferences (GSP) has concentrated on a relatively limited range of products. Around 50 percent of these preferential exports were dealt with by the EEC as sensitive or semi-sensitive products and were controlled through maximum quotas. The number of countries using the scheme are very few, the main beneficiaries being Yugoslavia, Hong Kong, Brazil, Korea, Malaysia and India, i.e. 55 percent of the total.

The application of preferential treatment is extremely limited and in 1980 only covered 60 percent of the maximum amount offered. The goods imported through the GSP only cover around 5 percent of the Community's total imports. Thus, the Community's scheme of preferences has done very little to achieve the objectives laid down in the UNCTAD's Resolution 21 (II) aimed at accelerating industrialization in developing countries.

The EEC countries continue to apply quantitive restrictions on imports which currently include 10 types of products, such as shoes, televisions, radios and spare parts, cutlery and plywood. Also included is trade in textiles through the GATT's Multi-fibre Agreement (MFA), which with each revision becomes more and more restrictive. The latest revision conceded differential treatment for major suppliers, in other words, it reinforced the already existing discrimination between countries. It cannot be denied that the EEC has taken considerable advantage of the MFA to steadily increase the protection given to the textile sector.

The Community indiscriminately applies safeguard clauses when any one of its industries is or appears to be threatened. The EEC, however, has insisted in the GATT that safeguards are only applied to those countries with the largest share of the Community's imports. This is another contributing factor to international discrimination on the part of the EEC and is particularly harmful to developing countries as this clause is applied more often than not to labour-intensive products, that is, products where these countries tend to have a comparative advantage.

Anti-dumping and countervailing duties are applied by the EEC in accordance with the GATT's norms without discriminating against those countries that have not signed the respective Codes, as is done in the United States. However, the tendency to resort to these measures is a way of increasing protectionism. From 1970 to 1975, only 20 cases of anti-dumping duties were processed but by 1980 the figure had increased to 31.

VI Trade between Mexico and the European Economic Community

As can be seen from the description provided in previous sections of this paper, Mexico is at a relative disadvantage compared to other countries in its trade relations with the European Economic Community. Exports from the EFTA, Mediterranean and ACP countries are given preference over those from Mexico. However, the discrimination is more theoretical than practical in that although Mexico's exports, like honey, tobacco and coffee, are faced with severe trade restrictions, Mexico really has no real trade problems with the European Economic Community.

This statement is the same as saying that the Upper Volta has no problems in its trade with Mexico. In both cases the reason why there are no problems is that trade relations are in fact minimal. Even if the European Economic Community were to lift the restrictions imposed on honey or any of the other products mentioned and retract its accusation to the effect that Mexican companies are exporting acrylic fibres to the

EEC at dumping prices, Mexico's exports to that region would still not increase significantly nor would this solve the country's commercial problems.

The problem arises when seen from a different angle, that is, not from the point of view of present transactions. Supposing that Mexico's exports to the EEC were to grow at a very fast rate, Mexico would then run into very serious problems with the Community, for as the number of products exported increased, so would the import restrictions placed on them by the EEC. Unlike the hypothetical export growth, the restrictions described earlier on in this paper are real and countries like Brazil, Argentina, Korea and Taiwan, amongst others, have already felt their effects. What we have proposed here as a hypothetical situation could become a reality should the Mexican Government's intention to promote non-petroleum exports come to fruition.

Over the last five years trade between Mexico and the EEC has suffered a major transformation. In 1979, Mexican exports to the region totalled 521 million US dollars, whilst imports from the EEC countries came to 2.513 billion US dollars leaving a deficit for Mexico of 1.632 billion dollars. After 1980 Mexican exports to the EEC underwent a major change as a result of the incorporation of oil as Mexico's main contribution to the Common Market. By 1983 these exports had reached 2.274 billion dollars and by 1984 they were at 2.7 billion. Mexico had gone from a 1.6 billion dollar deficit in 1981 to a 1.430 billion dollar surplus in 1984.

Eighty-five percent of Mexico's exports to the EEC are oil, so that if this is not taken into account in the total count, it would mean that the country's exports underwent zero growth between 1979 and 1984. Apart from oil exports, Mexico's positive trade balance is due to the strict adjustment process imposed by the Mexican authorities from 1982 on in response to the financial and economic crisis that broke out during that same year. These adjustments produced a 60 percent reduction in all imports from the Community between 1981 and 1984, around 1.260 billion dollars being the figure recorded for 1984.

Mexican exports to the EEC were made up mainly of 15 products with oil taking the largest share. Of the remaining 14, 5 are agricultural products (honey, coffee, cocoa, tobacco and cotton) and represent 4.15 percent of all Mexico's exports to the Common Market countries. Six are mineral products and account for 8.9 percent of the total. Ethylene accounts for 0.5 percent of the exports, while motor vehicles and auto spare parts represent 1.8 percent of total exports to the EEC.

Thus, one can see that only agricultural products, which represent less than 5 percent of Mexico's exports, could have problems in attaining access to the Common Market. Mineral products encounter no problems nor do motor vehicles and auto parts, most of which are exported to Germany from the Volkswagen Company in Mexico, which explains the absence of restrictions in this area. Therefore, export growth here depends basically on the trade policy adopted by the transnational company in question.

Mexico also exports to the EEC a number of chemical products, typewriters, electric cables, relays, parts for electronic valves, synthetic fibres, magnetic tapes, registers, micro-circuits and tractor parts, apart from raw materials such as tuna fish, garlic, grass fodder root, ixtle agave, canned asparagus, hemp rope, etc. However, the amount of these products exported is very small, although they could form the basis of future diversification in Mexico's products and markets.

On the other hand, the goods Mexico imports from the EEC are mainly composed of machinery for working metals, pipes, drain pipes and iron and steel connections, railroad vehicles and other capital goods. It can therefore be seen that the trading relationship between Mexico and the EEC is the classical one that exists between industrialized and developing countries.

With the aim of modifying this situation, the Council of the European Community and the Mexican Government drew up a Global Agreement on Economic Cooperation in 1975 whereby the contracting parties conferred most favored nation status on each other and promised to promote greater economic cooperation between themselves. This cooperation would involve bilateral trade in concrete projects designed to aid the development and diversification of trade itself. As part of this agreement, a mixed commission was created to examine the problems that might hinder reciprocal trade and to establish ways of promoting trade between the two parties.

There is no doubt as to the good intentions of both Mexico and the EEC to improve the institutional framework within which bilateral trade relations are carried out. This rapprochement made it possible for Mexico to introduce large quantities of oil into some of the Economic Community countries through bilateral agreements with certain countries. However, statistical data also show that in real terms the economic cooperation agreement has not been particularly effective in increasing Mexico's non-petroleum exports.

Mexico's inability to increase the volume of its exports has been due basically to two structural factors and another of a circumstancial nature. On the one hand, there has been very little interest on the part of the Mexican Authorities to promote export trade with the EEC and, on the other, it seems that Mexican exporters have always preferred the North American market as they consider it less risky than the European. When the Mexican Government made certain decisions concerning non-petroleum exports, it so happened that the US dollar was very over-valued in relation to other European currencies. As the Mexican peso slides according to the dollar, it became overvalued also in relation to the EEC currencies. Thus, Mexico's exports of some products to this market were reduced. Table 3 shows the extent to which the peso was overvalued in March 1985.

During the months that followed, the peso's overvaluation increased as the US dollar gained ground over the European currencies and the undervalued peso in relation to the US dollar managed to reduce the distance between them a little. The adjustment made to the exchange rate early in September put an end to the peso's overvaluation with regard to the European currencies.

To sum up, Mexican exports to the EEC have not increased due mainly to the government's trade policy which was aimed at catering to the domestic market and not to promoting exports. With the recent change in policy, Mexican exports will almost certainly grow. At that stage it is highly probable that the Community's restrictive measures will begin to have a negative effect on Mexican exports.

VII Mexico's Trade Policy

It is possible to identify several stages in Mexico's industrialization process according to GNP growth:
a) Import substitution of consumer goods from 1939 to 1960;

Table 3. Mexican peso's overvaluation in relation to some European currencies (March 1985)

Currency	Margin of overvaluation
French franc	6.5
German mark	13.3
British pound	20.8

Source: IMCE

b) Import substitution of intermediate products and durable consumer goods from 1960 to 1973;

c) Import substitution of capital goods and the first attempts to promote manufactured exports from 1970 to 1978;

d) Development of a leading sector from 1976 to 1982.

Each one of these stages is perfectly well defined in terms of the thrust given to economic growth in each case. If the thrust behind the growth were to wane, the country would lapse into the previous stage, although it is possible for stages to overlap. The first three stages comprise a well-defined model of import substitution at all costs. From the early seventies on, this model began to show signs of weakening but its ineffectiveness did not become evident until the mid-seventies.

As the import substitution scheme began to fade, it was substituted with a model based on a leading sector. At this point the oil sector became the axis of the country's economic development. The substitution of one model for another does not necessarily imply a drastic change in the country's trade policy. The average effective protection used in overall goods production went from 13 percent in 1960 to 18 percent in 1970, and then to 32 percent in 1980. However, by 1981 import substitution's contribution to the GNP was negative in almost 38 percent of the cases. On the other hand, exports' contribution to economic growth was around 5 percent due exclusively to oil exports. In all other sectors exports were either very insignificant or non-existent.

Oil exports increased the economy's buying power abroad, which led to a rapid growth in the imports needed to cover the precipitated growth in domestic demand, particularly with the directing of investment towards capital-intensive sectors. A rapid overvaluation of the Mexican currency from 1979 on also explains the particularly rapid growth in imports and the fact that imports from the EEC increased by 50 percent between 1979 and 1981.

However, this model suffered from one fundamental defect - the Mexican authorities had no way of controlling international oil prices. The subsequent fall in international oil prices sparked off the financial crisis which led to the economic crisis in 1982. Thus, under these circumstances the country was faced with three options. First, it could expand the import substitution model; second, it could keep up the leading sector model and combine it with the import substitution one; and third, it could search for a new development strategy designed to bring about a true structural change in the economy and prevent such serious economic crises from occurring in the future.

In the case of the first, expanding import substitution would involve a number of fundamental disadvantages. Firstly, there is very little room left for substituting imports, as may be observed in the low ratio of imports to total consumption in most sectors. Secondly, despite Mexico's 78 million inhabitants, its market is far too small for the economies of scale that would be necessary in the sectors where import substitution could still take place (the market would be about the same size as the Los Angeles or Greater New York area). The third drawback would be that if import substitution, i.e. basically of capital goods and "sophisticated" inputs, were to be expanded indiscriminately, it would lead to inefficiency which would extend both horizontally and vertically to the whole economy.

The second option would lead to the introduction of the undesirable elements of the two models, both of which have demonstrated their non-viability. It was for this reason that the Plan Nacional de Desarrollo (National Development Plan) and the Programa Nacional de Fomento Industrial y Comercio Exterior (National Program for Industrial Promotion and Foreign Trade) decided to seek a change in economic structure that would reach all sectors of the economy.

The basic instruments of this structural change were to be found in the encouragement of non-petroleum exports and a selective and efficient system of import substitution. It is interesting to note that the Plan Nacional de Desarrollo conferred trade policy with the task for which it was most suited, i.e. assigning productive resources to the different activities according to sectorial objectives. Trade policy would no longer be the guardian of the country's balance of payments, a task the PND entrusted to exchange policy and policies designed to control demand.

Both the PND and the PRONAFICE consider protection policy to be one of the most powerful tools available to the State for assigning productive resources. From this stems the need to rationalize protection. In 1981 effective protection had reached 48 percent, the highest level recorded since statistical data have been available on this indicator.

Economic policy has always been aimed at making best use of the domestic market at the expense of exports. Furthermore, excessive protection has encouraged capital-intensive production, a ridiculous situation in a country with an abundant labour force. With the elimination in July 1985 of the permits needed for 3,600 import fractions, together with another batch that had been liberated during the course of 1984, 90 percent of all fractions no longer require an import permit. This covers around two thirds of the country's total imports.

Trade liberalization was accompanied by a major modification to the exchange rate, i.e. 20 percent, and a new form of currency slide in which monetary flotation responds more precisely to variations in supply and demand, and the differentials between internal and external inflation could be compensated for. With this modification in exchange policy the peso's overvaluation in relation to the European currencies has been eliminated.

Not only has this measure made protection more transparent, and consequently made the rules of the game more clear both for producers and importers, but it has also managed to reduce effective protection dispersion. An added advantage lies in the fact that exporters have more precise criteria on which to base their decisions regarding investment and their choice between either local or foreign inputs. Therefore, although the bias against exports still exists, it has become less marked. Furthermore, the present protectionist structure gives reasonable protection to those sectors where import substitution can be carried out more effectively. The Mexican Government also published the Programa de Fomento Integral a las Exportaciones (Program for the Integrated Promotion of Exports) involving a series of measures designed to make the domestic market as profitable as the international one.

With systems like seasonal imports, drawback and joint exports, the exporter is in a position to choose his domestic and foreign suppliers, placing him on an equal footing with his international competitors. The terms and conditions of the financing the exporter receives are similar to those available in other exporting countries. And, by returning indirect taxes quickly to the end-exporter, the latter is no longer at a disadvantage in relation to his foreign competitors.

Lastly, a series of export incentives was established whereby exporters have the right to import goods necessary for their own productive activities or for those of their suppliers, but which require an import license. However, "DIMEX" effectiveness as an incentive has been diminished considerably as the number of products requiring import permits has fallen noticeably.

Thus the Mexican authorities have established favorable domestic conditions for effectively encouraging exports. It is clear that there is still much to be done as far as rationalizing protection is concerned, particularly in view of the fact that the range of tariffs is still fairly broad, going from 0 to 50 percent. Nonetheless, the efforts of the Mexican authorities to rationalize protection have been worthy of note.

These newly created conditions favoring exports will more than likely bring about a substantial increase in Mexican sales to the Community. It is then that the discrimination against Mexico present in the Community's trade policy will become more noticeable.

VIII The EEC's Direct Investment in Mexico

In 1940, 57.6 percent of all direct foreign investment (DFI) in Mexico was from the United States. This figure increased to 65.9 percent in 1965 and to 79.4 percent in 1970. During the seventies, however, direct investment by the United States underwent a relative reduction and by 1984 it had reached 66 percent. Investment by other countries increased significantly, particularly from West Germany, Switzerland and Japan.[13] During Mexico's economic boom from 1972 to 1981, Germany's share in total DFI went from 7.4 to 8.1 percent, while both France and the United Kingdom's share remained stable. The Netherlands, Belgium and Italy experienced a drop in their share of the DFI, although there was an increase in absolute terms. (See Table 4.)

With Mexico's economic crisis, DFI fell during 1982 and the outward flow of capital dropped 63 percent in relation to 1981. Alvarez Soberanis is of the opinion that this was caused mainly by a shortage of internal resources needed to back up foreign investment, which in turn meant a greater share of foreign capital in already established companies so as to draw in the resources needed to aid financial recovery. Furthermore, a large number of joint investment projects could not be undertaken as the percentage of local capital agreed upon in the corresponding contracts could not be raised owing to Mexico's limited financial capacity.

According to Alvarez Soberanis, currency foreign investment policy in Mexico contains 9 basic variables:

1.   DFI must be *complementary* to national investment both quantitively and qualitively.

2.   Selective promotion - DFI will be promoted in selected activities,

Table 4. Source of direct foreign investment (percentage of share)

Countries	1940	1970	1980	1984
United States	57.6	79.4	69.0	66.0
Germany	2.4	3.4	8.0	8.7
United Kingdom	8.6	3.3	3.0	3.1
France	2.2	1.6	1.2	1.8
Holland and Belgium	0.6	1.8	1.1	1.1
Italy	0.4	2.0	0.3	0.3
Japan	1.3	0.9	5.9	6.3

Source: J. Alvarez Soberanis, *op. cit.*

fields, sectors and products capable of generating foreign exchange and incorporating adequate technology.

3. Effective regulation - One of the policy's objectives is to guarantee the fulfilment of commitments made by companies with the National Foreign Investment Commission.

4. Diversification of sources - The aim here is to broaden Mexico's international economic relations so as to give the country the opportunity to chose the best investment options.

5. International economic cooperation - It is intended that advantage be taken of integrated economic and technical cooperation.

6. Technological contribution - The policy seeks to select DFI that offers the medium and high-technology the country requires, of good quality and at the right price. European technology is ahead in certain areas. For example, France leads in computing and communications, the United Kingdom in machinery and heavy industrial equipment and Germany in the chemical and pharmaceutical industry. Of all the contracts for technology transference registered at the Registro Nacional de Transferencia de Technología (National Register for Technology Transference), these three countries account for 15.7 percent.

7. Protection for production and employment - This stems from a casuistical analysis of the problem of companies using foreign capital as a result of current economic circumstances, and is aimed at finding solutions to their financial imbalance with a view to their remaining in Mexico at least while it is convenient to the country.

8. Promoting of local joint-investment - This is aimed at promoting joint-investment of Mexican capital in areas of the economy that most need activating and developing.

9. Administrative simplification - It is intended that all proposals for DFI be attended to as quickly as possible.

Mexico's economic recovery during 1984 was reflected in the flow of DFI which reached 1.442 billion US dollars and was mainly channelled into foreign companies already installed in Mexico. Forecasts for 1985 predict DFI of around 2 billion dollars, thus raising the total accumulated DFI to approximately 15 billion dollars. It would therefore appear that the flow of direct foreign investment is beginning to recover in Mexico.

The basis on which foreign investment has been carried out in Mexico in the past is however, undergoing certain modifications. One of the main attractions for DFI in Mexico has been the very high protectionist barriers introduced to stimulate domestic market development. Thus, direct foreign investment was established in a captive market and at most had to compete with local companies which often lacked the technology and the capital to be able to compete with these economically and technologically more powerful foreign companies. This does not necessarily imply that the foreign companies either absorbed or eliminated the ones based on local capital. In a number of sectors tacit "live and let live" agreements and market distribution arrangements were reached.

The new economic policy designed to encourage exports will allow Mexico to become more fully integrated into the international reconversion process currently underway, despite the limitations imposed on developing countries. Mexico's new DFI policy caters basically to the foreign market and not solely to the domestic market as it did in the past. Mexico's relative advantage in skilled labour will make it possible to establish new productive processes with foreign trade in mind. This phenomenon is already appearing in several of the country's productive sectors, such as the automobile industry, telecommunications and electronics.

Considering that the European Economic Community's total accumulated investment up to December 1984 was 1.932 billion dollars, one can assume that these countries will participate in the reconversion process on a large scale during the latter half of the decade. An additional attraction is the closeness of the North American market.

IX Conclusions

1. The European Economic Community as a whole is capable of growing between 3.5 and 4 percent during the next few years in view of the fact that it has managed to overcome the effects of inflation and it now must reduce its very high rate of unemployment. In the short-term less restrictive policies will probably be applied in several of these countries because of the coming elections. In the longer-term the Community's member countries will have to channel more economic resources into research investment and development if they wish to close the gap between them and the United States and Japan in this field. For example, the European Strategic Program for Research in Information Technology (ESPRIT) has a 5-year budget that does not even amount to the sum IBM has allocated to research and development in 1984 alone.

2. As Europe grows so will its imports. Further application of neo-protectionist measures will depend on whether a trade war arises

from the possible application of protectionist legislation on the part of the United States Congress.

3. It is unlikely that the countries of the Community would apply adjustment measures to those sectors where the comparative advantage has been passed on to developing countries. However, despite the measures introduced, the international reconversion process will continue due to the advantages that production in developing countries and industrial subcontracting represent for each individual company.

4. Be it through protectionist measures or a reduction in its fiscal deficit, the United States trade deficit must come down. This may occur with the outflow of capital in response to protectionist measures or due to a reduction in the fiscal deficit leading to a fall in interest rates. The dollar will tend to drop in value, thus making imports more attractive to the European Economic Community.

5. At the present time Mexico has virtually no trade problems with the EEC. However, should Mexican exports begin to grow and the number of different products sent to the EEC become more varied, they would soon come up against restrictions with the General System of Preferences, anti-dumping and countervailing duties, safeguard clauses as well as the restrictive measures inherent in the Common Agricultural Policy.

6. Mexico's new economic policy will give rise to increased imports from the EEC, although the growth rate of the same will be determined more by policies designed to control demand and by the country's monetary exchange policy.

7. In view of the economic recovery of the EEC countries and the international reconversion process, together with Mexico's new trade policy, European investment in Mexico can be expected to grow very rapidly during the next few years, but from now on it will be concentrated more on external markets.

Table 5. Mexico's trade balance with European Economic Community member countries (in thousands of dollars)

Country/block	1979	1980*	1981*	1982*	1983*	January November 1984*
West Germany						
Exports	213085	255954	213171	249497	269426	21532
Imports	821666	971955	1284878	913881	363834	38928
Balance	−608581	−716001	−1071707	−664384	−94408	−17396
Belgium-Luxemburg						
Exports	69-314	77277	66065	68857	57723	7868
Imports	127652	154730	123591	81053	46718	7748
Balance	−58338	−77453	−57526	−12196	+11005	+120
Denmark						
Exports	8560	2197	5082	2100	8002	441
Imports	26052	28952	35767	43816	19084	1041
Balance	−17492	−26755	−30685	−41716	−11082	−599
France						
Exports	71679	566781	931298	940993	832347	87800
Imports	516006	520438	621289	349336	359113	23703
Balance	−444327	−46343	−310009	+591657	+473234	+64096
Ireland						
Exports	656	1787	487	308	360	50
Imports	36738	65128	85290	21180	5765	1938
Balance	−36082	−63341	−84803	−20872	−5405	−1881
Italy						
Exports	56423	100586	102634	391910	149355	30229
Imports	246653	305169	461736	431773	166842	19918
Balance	−190230	−204583	−359102	−39863	−17487	+10310

Netherlands						
Exports	46199	76295	65580	19301	39875	3315
Imports	92447	98472	169979	103129	60616	4768
Balance	−46248	−22177	−104399	−83828	−20741	−1453
United Kingdom						
Exports	45086	43503	244741	944885	915437	95556
Imports	282858	405042	444774	287032	170254	17389
Balance	−237772	−361539	−200033	−666853	+745183	+78166
Greece						
Exports	10178	10093	18628	1014	1354	329
Imports	2858	6826	19850	1035	23	235
Balance	+7320	+3267	−1222	−21	+1331	+93
European Economic Community						
Exports	521180	1134473	1647686	2618865	2273879	247129
Imports	2152930	2556712	3247154	2223235	1192249	115672
Balance	−1631750	−1422239	−1599468	+395630	+1081630	+131456

* Preliminary figures
Note: Greece has been included as an EEC member as from 1979 so that the statistics will be comparative, even though it entered the Community in 1980
Source: IMCE

28

Notes

1. Maddison, Angus, "Naturaleza y causas del estancamiento económico: un exámen de siete paises", *Comercio Exterior*, Vol. 35, No.6 (June 1985), Mexico, pp. 593-603.
2. *Ibid.*
3. De Mateo, Fernando, "Políticas económicas y ajustes del tipo de cambio", Year V, Vol. 1, No.23 (July-September1982).
4. De Ghellinck, Elizabeth, "La política industrial de la Comunidad Económica Europea", *Comercio Exterior*, Vol. 35, No.7, Mexico, July 1985, pp. 665-671.
5. *Ibid.* p. 669.
6. See for example, "A Community strategy to develop Europe's industry", Brussels, October 1981.
7. Treaty of Rome, Article 39.
8. European Economic Community Commission, "Europe's Common Agricultural Policy", February, 1981.
9. EEC Commission,"Orientaciones para fortalecer als relaciones entre la CCE y América Latina", *Comercio Exterior*, Vol. 35, No.6 (June 1985), Mexico.
10. *Ibid*, p. 605.
11. Parts of this section are based on S. Reichenbach, *op. cit.*
12. In 1983 preferential imports from Mexico were restricted in the case of only one out of 132 products subject to quotas during that year.
13. Alvarez Soberanis, Jaime, "Consideraciones sobre la inversión de la CEE en México", *Comercio Exterior,* Vol. 35, No.6, Mexico, June 1985, pp. 371-377.

Co-operation between the European Economic Community (EEC) and Latin America - with Special Reference to Mexico: A European View

PETER COFFEY

The Background

Until recently, the European Economic Community (EEC), despite the conclusion of a number of bi-lateral agreements with some individual Latin American countries,[1] had given the impression that it regarded Latin America as a kind of forgotten continent. Indeed, since its inception, ongoing official trade and co-operation agreements have been made exclusively with African and Mediterranean countries. Most interestingly of all, there has never any bi-lateral trade agreement between the Community and the United States.

Fortunately, more recently, under the influence of Commissioner Wilhelm Haferkamp, and now, very hopefully, with the active interest and encouragement of the new Commissioner, Claude Cheysson, there are signs that the EEC is developing a deeper interest in the affairs of Central and Latin America. We shall return to this theme at the end of this paper.

Despite the Community's continuous interest in developing its relations with African countries (now extended to the ACP States) and its former apparent lack of interest in Latin America, the links with the latter are important. Thus, in 1982, trade between the two sides accounted for 16.9 percent of Latin America's and 5.2 percent of the Community's total trade. Furthermore, the EEC has generally experienced a deficit (substantial since 1982) in its balance-of-payments with Latin American countries. However, before going into greater detail about these matters, at this stage, it is useful to examine the principles which govern the Community's trade policies, and, the ways, apart from specific bi-lateral agreements, by which Latin American countries can improve their trade and other links with the EEC.

The European Economic Community (EEC) - The Seven Principles

The EEC is a highly integrated customs union and a de-facto monetary union consisting of twelve West European countries. The Community is the world's most important trading bloc.

In a recent work,[2] the author has identified the following seven principles as forming the basis of the external economic relations of the EEC:

1. The EEC (with the exception of the United Kingdom and its supplies of North Sea oil and coal reserves in that and some other countries) is not self-sufficient in supplies of energy and raw materials. Therefore, these commodities have generally been allowed to enter the Community either free of duty or with very low tariffs.

2. At the end of the transitional period, the Common External Tariff (CET) would consist of the average of the existing (1975) tariffs of the Member States. Subsequent participation by the EEC in a series of international trade negotiations has resulted in a rather low average CET.

3. It was agreed that special arrangements would be made for existing overseas territories, dependencies and the like for which Member States exercised responsibility. This policy has evolved over time for the special arrangements made for such countries to the two Yaoundé Agreements and further on to the present Third Lomé Agreement.

4. At the outset, the Community decided to embark upon the construction of a Common Agricultural Policy (CAP) and until the Common Agricultural Market (CAM) actually came into being the EEC was unwilling to discuss the question of agricultural matters in international trade negotiations. Since the full achievement of the CAM, its existence has tended to negatively influence the Community's trade relations with most parts of the world - especially with Eastern Europe, Australasia and Latin America.

5. The Community expressed its willingness to enter into international trade negotiations with non-Community countries. Subsequently, the EEC has been (together with the USA and more recently - Japan) the principal protagonist in point 2, and following the Tokyo Round Negotiations, the average CET is now rather low.

6. Partly as a consequence of the low CET and partly due to the increased competitive ability of a growing number of Third World countries (particularly in the fields of clothing and textiles) the EEC has, since the 1970s increasingly resorted to non-tariff barriers of a "voluntarist" nature which are sometimes described as Orderly Marketing

Arrangements (OMAs) or Voluntary Export Restrictions (VERs). Currently, efforts are being made to "persuade" Japan to restrict exports of cars and electronic products to EEC Member States.

7.   Since the mid 1970s, the Community has started to move in the direction of attempting to secure its supplies of energy and raw materials.[3] This more recent policy is an obvious reaction to the lack of selfsufficiency in these fields - which was mentioned in point 1.

Although these basic principles do clearly explain the Community's trading attitudes and policies towards imports and exports of agricultural products, raw materials and some 'sensitive' products, they do not necessarily explain the choice or lack of choice of policies for specific geographical areas - about which so much has been written. Therefore, it is useful to examine such areas for which policies have or have not been made.

When examining these principles, it is important to bear in mind that the internal economic policies of the EEC are at least as important (notably the CAP) as the official external economic policies in influencing relations between the Community and third parties. Furthermore, there are still areas of cultural, economic and technological activity that are still much more the responsibility of the individual Member States than of the Community. Indeed, in the specific fields of cultural affairs and capital investment, the EEC has defined no policy for third parties.

Relations between the EEC and Latin America - with Special Reference to Mexico

Economic and political relations between the two sides take place at two levels, at the Community-Mexico level and at a bilateral (Mexico-Member State) level.

The EEC, in the person of the Commission, is responsible for the trade relations of the individual Member States vis-à-vis third parties. Here, one may say that each country in the Common Market has transferred most of its sovereignty concerning trade policy to the Community. This fact is underlined by the Commission's role as the negotiator for the whole Community in international trade negotiations and by the acceptance by Member States of the inclusion of a "Community Clause" in all trade agreements. Also, all the Community's trade policies are very much influenced by its internal economic policies.

In the case of a country like Mexico, economic relations with the Community are developed mainly in four ways:

(i) through multinational trade negotiations, following the implementation of the agreements reached in the Tokyo Round, the Community's average CET is rather low
(ii) through the generalised system of preferences (GSPs)
(iii) through the Multi-Fibre Agreement (MFA), and
(iv) through specific agreements with the country concerned. In the specific case of Mexico, the EEC's official relations have reached a particularly formal level.

The Record

In recent years, and despite the negative influence of the Community's Common Agricultural Policy (CAP), trade between the two sides has steadily increased. Interestingly enough, between 1978 and 1982, the Community's imports from Latin America have increased whereas those from ACP countries have declined. More specifically, 91 percent of Latin America's exports to the Community (see Table 1 for detailed breakdown) are made up of raw materials and agri-food products. In contrast, 85 percent of the EEC's exports to Latin America consist of industrial manufactures.

These statistics deserve further examination since they may tend to confirm the worst fears of some of our Latin American friends. Certainly, in the case of agricultural and tropical products, one suspects that the levies and duties of the CAP together with the preferences accorded to ACP countries have influenced the performance of Latin America countries - though the generally negative international economic climate will also have played a role here. In the specific case of Mexico, and in contrast with Brazil, it seems that a full use of the possible quotas

Table 1. Latin America's (20 countries) exports to the EEC (as a percentage of total)

	1978	1982
1. Agricultural products (except tropical)	33.2	24.1
2. Tropical products	25.4	17.2
3. Raw materials	14.3	13.0
4. Processed products	20.6	19.2
5. Mineral fuels	5.2	24.8

Source: EC Commission, January 1984.

under both the GSPs and the MFAs has not been made. In 1981, Mexico only made 59 percent effective use of the GSPs.

In contrast with the afore-mentioned record, the upsurge in EEC imports of minerals and petroleum products can only be to the benefit of a country like Mexico.

As has already been mentioned, capital investment flows are still the prerogative of the individual Member States of the EEC. Thus, this particularly important area of economic interest is still conducted on a bi-lateral nation-state basis, although the Community as a bloc competes with the United States for first place as an international investor in Latin America. Perhaps the Community's guarantee for the $ 600 million loan for the Carajas Iron Ore project, in Brazil, marks the beginning of a real EEC presence in the field of capital investment?

The EEC and Mexico: The Real Situation

On 16 September 1975, a Co-operation Agreement[4] was signed in Brussels between Mexico and the European Economic Community. The two parties granted each other the "most-favoured nation treatment" over a particularly wide range of matters and expressed the desire to encourage commercial and economic co-operation "in all sectors of interest to them so as to contribute to their economic and social progress and to the balance of their reciprocal trade at the highest possible level taking into account Mexico's special situation as a developing country."

To facilitate the successful implementation of the agreement, a Joint Committee was set up, composed of representatives of both parties.

To the author, this agreement is much too general in scope and quality. There is nothing specific about it and the impression is given that this is the kind of general co-operation agreement that the Community could have signed with any country.

In comparison, the new agreement with Brazil is both broader in scope and deeper in quality. It defines specific areas, e.g. in technology, where there should be co-operation between the two sides. The author would like to see the agreement with Mexico transformed into something similar to that made with Brazil.

The necessity of expanding trade and investment flows between the EEC and Mexico is clearly underlined by the following statistics. When examining these figures it should be borne in mind that trade and investment flows for the Community and Brazil show that the EEC is that

country's most important trading partner and its most important source
of capital investment.

The EEC exports mainly machinery and professional, scientific and
other instruments to Mexico. In turn, the Community imports mainly
petroleum and related products plus non-ferrous metals from Mexico.
To a lesser degree, there are also imports of crude fertilizers, minerals,
sugar, organic chemicals, vegetables and fruit.

The composition of Mexico's exports to the EEC (and to other parts
of the world) with the heavy reliance on petroleum and related products
(74.8 percent of total exports in 1983) offers an explanation as to why
(especially when compared with similar countries) she has not been able
to take much advantage of important EEC concessions in the field of the
Generalised System of Preferences. Equally, relatively slight concessions are enjoyed in the framework of the Multi-Fibres Agreement.[5]

Since the United States is Mexico's main trading partner, it is logical
that that country constitutes the main source of foreign investment - at
the end of 1983 American investment constituted a massive 68 percent of
the total. Among the Common Market countries (as in a number of
other Latin American countries) West Germany was the main investor
providing 8 percent of the total. In comparison, the United Kingdom
provided only 2.8 percent.

Possible Future Policies

According to the author, the best way whereby Mexico could deepen
and widen her relations with the EEC would be to diversify the structure
of her own economy. According to certain reports recently received in
Western Europe,[6] the Mexican Government is trying to do precisely this.

Table 2. Mexico's main trading partners in 1983 (Percentage of total)

	Exports	Imports
USA	58.1	63.4
EEC	10.4	15.0
Japan	7.0	4.6
LAIA	4.1	2.5
Brazil	3.0	1.8
Spain	1.3	2.1

Source: Lloyds Bank International

If these plans are successful, then it would be much easier to more fully utilise the concessions given by the Community. Also, there would be stronger grounds for negotiating a more far-reaching agreement between the two sides. In turn, more capital investment would be likely to flow to Mexico from the Common Market - at all levels. Last, but not least, this would encourage a greater use by Mexico of the ECU[7] - both for trade and loan purposes. This would be a much more balanced manner of building Mexico's future economic structure.

Table 3. The new composition of the ECU.

	As a percentage of the total	In National Currencies
Deutsche Mark	32	10.719
French Franc	19	1.31
Pound Sterling	15	0.0878
Italian Lira	10.2	140
Dutch Guilder	10.1	0.256
Belg. Franc	8.2	3.71
Danish Kronor	2.7	0.219
Greek Drachma	1.3	1.15
Irish Pound	1.2	0.00871
Lux. Franc	0.3	0.16

Notes

1. These general bi-lateral agreements are:
   - the EEC - Brazil Trade Agreement of 1974 which entered into force on 1. October of the same year. This Agreement has now been replaced by a Co-operation Agreement, signed on 18. September 1980, and which came into force on 1. October, 1982.
   - An Agreement for commercial and economic co-operation between the EEC and Mexico which was signed on 15. July, 1975 and which came into force on 1. November of the same year.
   - A Non-preferential Trade Agreement between the EEC and Uruquay came into force on 1. August, 1974.
2. See: P. Coffey, *Main Economic Policy Areas of the EEC*, Nijhoff, Den Haag, 1983.
3. The most important statement here was that made by the Commission in "The Supply with Raw Materials of the EEC", Supplement of the Bulletin of the European Communities, No.1/75. This statement called for the "securing" of the Community's supplies of energy and raw materials. Since the publication of this statement, the Commission has since made a number of similar calls.
4. Agreement for Commercial and Economic Co-operation between the EEC and Mexico. Official Journal, L.274/75.

5. The MFA concessions for Mexico cover only a limited number of products. However, in each case, the quantities of Mexican imports allowed into the EEC is quite substantial.
6. Notably in an article: "Mexico buys some breathing space", which appeared in the *Financial Times*, 14 March 1985.
7. The ECU or the European Currency Unit is the official unit of account of the European Communities and is composed of the Community currencies in the following manner (since 16 September 1984):

PART 2

THE DEBT QUESTION

Latin American Foreign Debt and the International Financial System*

HEINZ GERT PREUSSE

1. Introduction

For a long time the scarcity of capital has been identified as one of the major obstacles to economic development. It appears to be quite natural, therefore, that developing countries (LDCs) used to rely on capital inflows to avoid capital shortage and foster growth and development. It is equally important to note that with production capacity rising during a successful development process the creditworthiness usually increases and additional capital inflows will be attracted. Total foreign debt may rise substantially and progressively during this process without doing harm to the country's ability to serve this debt as long as the funds are used productively (Kharas, 1984, 419).

It is, therefore, not sufficient to point to rising foreign debt ratios to demonstrate a debt problem. Rather, increasing foreign debt may very well be the result of successful development performance "due to high rates of return to capital and appropriate financial and exchange rate policies" (Mehdi Zaidi, 1985, 574). Thus, high and increasing foreign debt has been characteristic for last century's "newly industrializing countries", namely the USA, Canada and Australia, it was also familiar to Latin American development in the 60s (the LA current account deficit amounted to an average of 17 % between 1966 -73) and "Brazil's economic miracle in particular was characterized by ... debt-led growth" (Fishlow, 1985, 100).

* Paper presented at the Conference TOWARDS A EUROPEAN FOREIGN PO-LICY, Colloquium organised to celebrate the 25th anniversary of the Europa Institute and the 20th anniversary of the International Course in European Integration, University of Amsterdam, Amsterdam, 12-13 December 1985.

However, after the first oil price increase in 1973, LDC long term debt accumulated at unprecedented rates from 135,4 billion US $ in 1974 to 301,2 bil. US $ in 1978. For 1985, World Bank estimates are at 710 bil. US $ and an amount of 880 bil. US $ is to be expected if short term debt and the use of IMF credit facilities is included (World Bank 1985, IX, XI). This outcome has been attributed to the fact, that LDCs as a whole and the major LA borrowers in particular relied on quite similar strategies to cope with the two oil price shocks of the seventies. They increased foreign lending in order to sustain a stable growth process despite the drastic deterioration of the terms-of-trade and they trusted in increased future debt servicing capacity to manage the accumulating debt burden. While this strategy proved to be successful until 1978 and LDCs became a stabilizing element in the world economy, it failed when applied a second time after 1979.

In 1982 the international debt crisis became visible when Mexico had to reschedule 49 bil. US $ of its debt to commercial banks. In 1983 and 1984, Brazil, Venezuela and Argentina, the three other major LA borrowers, were to follow (together with an increasing number of smaller countries). Up to now, a definite case of national insolvency could be prevented by a number of ad hoc crisis managements which have been called somewhat euphorically "the cooperative international strategy" (Morgan Guaranty Trust, 1985). Crisis management has been successful so far and it has been urgently needed, "in order to gain time to correct faulty developments on a durable basis; but we should not succumb to the illusion that crisis management itself is the solution" (Pöhl, 1983). This is to say that if it is legitimate for developing countries to import real resources to stimulate future growth, the debt problem cannot said to be solved just because insolvency is (temporarily) avoided. On the contrary, another requirement has to be met: debt servicing should not, in the medium and long run, effect the debtor country's ability to grow. Introducing this additional condition opens up a number of important questions of national and international economic policy. In what is to follow I will discuss some aspects of the debt problem with special reference to Latin America.

2. Capital Inflows and Economic Growth

From the capital importing country's point of view the use of external resources should facilitate a push of national GDP growth rates in such a way as to permit future debt servicing out of the additional income generated through the productive employment of the external resources. The determination of an adequate debt burden based on this consideration can be regarded as some kind of an economy-wide investment problem under uncertainty. As such, the success of foreign lending is open to changes of the factors which determine the efficiency of the development programme. Furthermore, the evaluation of the data itself may be faulty so that the whole program was likely to fail from the very beginning. Emphasizing this investment aspect of international lending allows to distinguish between two major problem areas.

Firstly, changes in the international environment pose a permanent threat (and a chance) to the actual performance of the economy. This is the case, for example, when the international economy suffers from an extended period of depression, so that export prospects become cloudy and terms-of-trade (eventually) deteriorate. Such kinds of macro disturbances, however, are very often accompanied or even caused by external shocks which might change relative prices in the long run.

Both events are characteristic features of the international economic events during the past decade. However, cyclical downswings and permanent changes of relative prices need quite different policy responses. The former may be attached by conventional demand management, the latter, instead, need to be corrected by adequate adjustments of productive capacity. To the extent that a country does not manage to adjust to the changing international environment, international competitiveness deteriorates and the rate of return to capital employed in national ventures decreases.

Secondly, there may be an inadequate use of capital inflows in the importing country itself, so that the rate of return on capital falls short of the plannings. This threat to future debt servicing capacity appears to be especially pronounced in countries which suffer from internal economic and political instability and which persistently sustain a highly distorted incentive system.

Just another form of inadequate use of external credit takes place, if it is used to raise the national consumption level instead of adding to productive ventures. In as much as capital inflows are used to substitute for national savings (in the case of a saving constraint) or imports of consumer goods are increased (in the case of a foreign exchange constraint), no additional income is likely to be generated and future debt servicing has to be financed out to an unchanged GDP.[1] As regards the debt servicing capacity, credit financing of current expenditure and misallocation of investable funds appear to be almost equivalent. In both cases the return on total capital inflows will be negatively effected and the servicing of debt out of increased GDP becomes doubtful.

It is worthwhile noting that external and internal factors are closely interrelated in reality. Thus, if external economic conditions are changing, what has proved to be a successful strategy in the past may suddenly become obsolete. However, any particular country can minimize the negative effects imposed from changes on the world market if it provides an economic framework conducive to flexible adjustment. If this is the case, efforts to improve the national economic conditions and measures to increase foreign financial assistance can - at least partly - be seen as substitutes.

3. Reflections on the Current Debt Crisis

In most of the projections of future debt scenarios a 3 % growth rate of GNP on a world-wide level has been used as some kind of a magic figure which would allow developing countries to solve the debt crisis on their own. Cline, who used especially optimistic parameter values (De Gregorio, 1985, 15) even named a critical threshold of 2,5 - 3 % for OECD growth. "... most major countries would show substantial improvement in balance of payments and relative debt burden and ... by the late 1980s, debt-export ratios would be back to levels previously associated with creditworthiness" (Cline, 1985, 186). Dornbusch/Fischer (1984), Fishlow (1985) and the Inter-American Development Bank (IDB) (1985) criticize Cline's optimistic view. While Dornbusch/Fischer are more pessimistic as to the scope for an improvement of the international economic conditions and its effects on Latin America in particular, Fishlow and the IDB also emphasize the burden imposed on Latin American economies out of the existing debt obligations. They claim that existing rescheduling arrangements imply a net transfer of resources from Latin America to the industrialized world which cannot be financed along with essential imports. However, when future growth prospects are hindered because of actual debt servicing obligations another vicious circle of poverty may result:

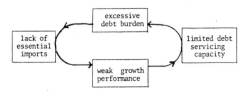

Recent data (Morgan Guaranty Trust (MGT), World Financial Markets, Sept./Oct. 1985; Inter-American Development Bank, 1985 Report) appear to support the more pessimistic views of the problem (Tables 1-4). In 1985 world economic recovery did not keep pace with the 1984

Table 1. Economic growth

	Real GDP growth percent per annum		Percent change in GDP per capita from 1980-81 peak to 1985
	1984	1985	
Argentina	2.0	—4.0	—17.1
Brazil	4.5	5.0	—5.6
Chile	6.3	1.0	—14.4
Ecuador	4.1	2.5	—6.3
Mexico	3.5	2.5	—9.4
Peru	4.5	3.5	—13.7
Venezuela	—1.8	0.5	—17.1

Source: Morgan Guaranty Trust, World Financial Markets, Sept./Oct. 1985.

Table 2. Trade and current account performance cumulative balances, in billions of dollars

	Merchandise trade balance		Current account balance	
	1980—1982	1983—1985	1980—1982	1983—1985
Argentina	2.1	11.7	—11.8	—7.0
Brazil	—0.8	31.8	—40.8	—7.5
Chile	—3.4	2.0	—9.0	—4.7
Ecuador	0.6	3.0	—2.8	—0.6
Mexico	—1.4	34.0	—26.0	9.3
Peru	—0.1	2.3	—3.3	—1.5
Venezuela	18.8	20.5	4.5	10.3

Source: Morgan Guaranty Trust, World Financial Markets, Sept./Oct. 1985.

growth rate of 5 %. OECD real GNP growth will hardly exceed 2,5 % this year and it is unlikely to do so in 1986 (MGT, 1985, 4). Equally disappointing are real GDP growth rates for six of the seven major LA debtor countries. Only Brazil managed to increase GDP growth slightly to 5 % according to MGT data. Recent data published by the German Council of Economic Advisors also estimate the Brazilian GDP growth rate below the 1984 value of 4,5 % (Sachverständigenrat, Jahresgutach-

Table 3. Net capital outflows[1] average annual flows, billions of dollars minus sign denotes net outflows

	1977-80	1981-82	1983-84
Argentina	—3.39	—6.95	—0.24
Brazil	—0.88	0.15	—1.78
Chile	0.13	—0.18	0.35
Ecuador	—0.37	0.12	—0.22
Mexico	—4.00	—8.21	—6.51
Peru	—0.08	0.45	—0.52
Venezuela	—2.06	—7.24	—2.64

1. Derived as a residual of current account balance, net foreign direct investment flows, changes in external debt, and changes in official reserves and in the foreign assets of domestic banks.

Source: Morgan Guaranty Trust, World Financial Markets, Sept./Oct. 1985.

Table 4.

	Debt-to-export ratios average of gross external debt at beginning and end of year as percent of exports of goods and services			Interest payments-to-export ratios scheduled interest payments as percent of exports of goods and services		
	1982	1984	1985	1982	1984	1985
Argentina	405	473	483	50	56	52
Brazil	339	322	368	54	38	41
Chile	333	402	442	44	44	46
Ecuador	240	250	254	30	30	24
Mexico	299	293	322	44	37	33
Peru	251	330	370	25	33	31
Venezuela	169	177	201	18	16	18

Source: Morgan Guaranty Trust, World Markets, Sept./Oct. 1985.

ten 1985, 19). Consequently, the debt scenario has darkened again compared to the slightly more optimistic situation registered in 1984. Foreign debts have continued to climb and so have debt-export ratios. Even the interest payments-to-export ratios have not declined significantly in most countries. The reason is that real interest rates remain at an exceptionally high level despite the drastic decrease of nominal rates since mid-1982 (the six month dollar LIBOR dropped from nearly 16 to about 8 %). For the ten debtor countries as a whole it is most interesting to note, that the improvements in trade balances are mainly due to import savings. Again Brazil forms a notable exception. Its growth rate of exports exceeded 10 % 1983 and 1984, but dropped to - 3,5 % in 1985 (Table 5). Even in this particular case, both debt and interest payments-to-export ratios have increased. The potentially negative impact of the 1985 developments is reflected in the corrected projection for the development of debt/export ratios for three main debtor countries (Chart 1). The trends in debt ratios based on the 1985 figures are significantly less promising than those calculated on the basis of the 1983 situation.

Given the relatively unfavourable development of the international debt situation this year and the uncertain prospects for economic growth in the industrialized countries, two major strategies to overcome the debt problem will most probably be discussed intensively again in the near future.

Proponents of the first strategy will put emphasis on the international market and the possibilities to improve the international financial system. Those who concentrate on the second strategy will probably stress LDCs' own capacity to adapt their national economic policies to meet the challenge of international markets and to fight domestic deficiencies. They would question the validity of the vicious circle of indebtedness outlined above.

Unfortunately, it is an especially difficult undertaking to give a serious statement on the adjustment capacity of different LDCs without going into detailed studies of particular country experiences. Let me, instead, try to outline some stylized aspects of the experience with development efforts in LA countries in the recent past. This should not at all be taken as a substitute for more deep-rooted country studies, but it may contribute to the discussion of the problem.

To begin with, the scope for an improvement of national economic development performance can said to be the greater the worse the actual economic strategy, works. What could be an appropriate meter to evaluate a country's economic strategy, however? How could one

Table 5. Economic situation in highly indebted developing countries

Country	GDP[1][2]				Consumer prices[2]				Public deficit[3]			
	1982	1983	1984	1985[7]	1982	1983	1984	1985[7]	1982	1983	1984	1985[7]
Argentina	−4,6	+2,8	+1,9	−2	+165,2	+344,2	+626,7	+700	−7,1	−17,5	−10,2	−4½
Brazil	+0,9	−3,2	+4,5	+4	+98,0	+142,0	+196,7	+210	−15,8	−16,6	−23,5	−28
Mexico	−0,6	−5,3	+3,5	+3	+59,0	+101,8	65,5	+50	−15,4	−8,5	−6,2	−4
Venezuela	+0,7	−5,6	−1,1	+2	+9,6	+6,3	12,2	+15	−5,3	−1,5	+3,5	1
Indonesia	+2,2	+4,2	+5,8	+3	+9,5	+11,8	+10,5	+7½	−2,4	−1,5	+3,0	−2
Philippines	+1,9	+1,3	−5,3	+½	+10,2	+10,0	+50,3	+27½	−4,2	−1,7	−1,4	−1½
South Korea	+5,5	+9,5	+7,6	+3½	+7,3	+3,4	+2,3	+2½	−3,1	−1,1	−1,4	−2

Country	Exports[2][4]				Current account[4][5]				Interest payments/exports[6]			
	1982	1983	1984	1985[7]	1982	1983	1984	1985[7]	1982	1983	1984	1985[7]
Argentina	−16,6	+2,8	+3,4	+7½	−2,4	−2,4	−2,5	−1½	51,7	56,9	54,8	55½
Brazil	−13,3	+8,6	+23,3	−3½	−16,3	−6,8	+0,0	−½	53,5	42,2	37,9	39½
Mexico	+6,5	+5,1	+7,8	+2½	−6,2	+5,3	+4,0	+2	44,3	41,6	37,2	33
Venezuela	−18,2	−10,8	+8,8	+2	−4,2	+4,4	+5,0	+1½	21,0	23,2	24,4	21½
Indonesia	−15,4	−5,4	+11,0	−4	−5,3	−6,3	−2,1	−3		.		
Philippines	−12,3	−0,3	+7,7	+4	−3,2	−2,8	−1,3	−1	24,9	21,9	27,6	28
South Korea	+1,0	+11,1	+13,5	+6	−2,7	−1,6	−1,4	−1	12,7	10,6	11,0	11

1) constant prices
2) percent change from preceding year
3) public budget as percent of GDP
4) goods, in US $
5) billion US $ (surplus: +, deficit: —)
6) not directly comparable because of conceptual differences
7) own estimation based on international orgnizations

Source: Council of Economic Advisors, 1985 Report to the Government of the Federal Republic of Germany based on data received from international organizations

Chart 1. Debt/export ratios for Argentina, Brasil and Mexico. Early 1983 projection (A) versus September 1985 projection (B).

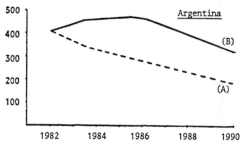

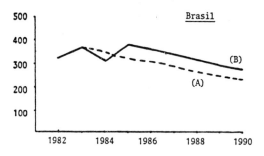

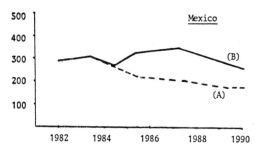

separate those events that are in fact controlled by national economic policy from those to be attributed to the world market? We do not have a definite answer to these questions and in the literature on this subject a series of different answers can be found. Two statements on the causes of the development of foreign debt after the second oil price increase may be illustrative.

Wiesner (1985) finds that "the debt crisis can be traced back to a fiscal disequilibrium, and ultimately to an unresolved political struggle between competing groups that wanted to have a large share of income" (p. 191). He employs IMF savings and investment data on Argentina,

Brazil, and Mexico (Table 6) to show that gross domestic investment and national savings have decreased quickly since 1980 while external savings increased until 1982 (Mexico: 1981). This observation leads to the conclusion that "since the accumulation of external debt was growing at a faster pace than the accumulation of productive investment, a debt crisis was just a question of time ..." (p. 192).

Fishlow (1985, 107-111), on the other hand, looked at the problem from a different point of view. He shows that LDCs reacted to the second oil price shock by trying to repeat the successful strategy of growth-led debt employed up to 1978. However, this time industrial countries mainly resisted the temptation to start another round of inflationary adjustment and accepted a deep and lasting depression. As a result, developing countries' exports and terms-of-trade suffered for an extended time period and the real rate of interest jumped up. Fishlow quantified the effects of the higher oil-price, the recession-induced reduction in export earnings and the higher interest rates on the current account of Nonoil Exporting Developing Countries. He concludes that in the absence of these three events the current account of these countries would have shown a deficit of 11,8 bil. US $ in 1982 compared to the actual deficit of 86,8 bil. US $ (Fishlow, 1985, 108). Nevertheless, it would be wrong "to blame the oil-price and recession shocks alone" (p. 110) for the actual development of current account deficits. Even the adjusted deficit would have risen to around 70 bil. US $ in 1980 and

Table 6. Savings and investment (as percent of GDP)

	1980	1981	1982	1983
Argentina				
Gross domestic investment	25.7	20.0	18.1	17.1
National savings	22.6	16.2	13.0	13.3
External savings	3.1	3.8	5.0	3.8
Brazil				
Gross domestic investment	21.1	19.2	18.4	15.0
National savings	16.0	15.1	12.9	12.0
External savings	5.1	4.1	5.5	3.0
Mexico				
Gross domestic investment	28.1	29.0	21.2	16.5
National savings	24.0	23.2	17.8	20.2
External savings	4.1	5.8	3,4	-3.7

Source: International Monetary Fund.

1981, mainly due to particular domestic economic policy strategies in some major Latin American debtor countries. During this period Mexico advanced to one of the leading oil exporters and the Mexican Government as well as foreign creditors estimated the future debt servicing capacity to be practically unlimited. Based on these prospects the Mexican Government initiated a striking new developing program (the industrial plan) without paying adequate attention to its inherent risks. This argument applies to the strategy itself (Dutch disease),[2] but also to the careless evaluation of the future situation on the international oil markets. Meanwhile, Argentina and Chile had liberalized their financial markets according to monetarist rules without paying due attention to the inherent dynamics of monetary disturbances. Begged by an undeclared but widely believed and ultimately practised "de facto socialization of the banking system" (Díaz-Alejandro, 1985, 1) capital inflows were abnormally high and ultimately strangled national growth.

Drawing on data from IDB these three countries alone accumulated current account deficits of 14,818.1 millions of US $ in 1980 and of 23,386.2 mil. US $ in 1981 (IDB, 1985, Table 41).

Leaving aside these three cases of misspecified national economic policies, which have - interestingly enough - been based on quite different ideologies one still has to face the broader question of the lessons to be learned from the experiences of the recent debt crisis.

Obviously the policy measures which are to be applied to cope with the problems of changing world trade and financial conditions are pre-determined by the country's judgement on the role the world market will have to play within its national development strategy. Ignoring these changes would only be the right answer to existing problems if the costs of isolation could be estimated to be less than those which have to be borne by a country that is in need of structural adjustment to (permanently) changing international conditions (Hesse, Keppler, Preusse, 1985, 6). After the experiences with extended Latin American import substitution strategies, on the one hand, and with the sound economic success of those countries, which offensively use the chances offered by large and open markets and by improved access to cheap foreign technologies on the other, it is hard to believe that inward looking strategies (except at the very beginning of the industrial development process) are an appropriate solution for those countries that try to catch up with the industrialized world. This widely taken view is also shared by most governments in Latin American countries today (Quito declaration). The question: How much national economic policy in Latin American countries has already contributed to the solution of the international debt crisis? can, therefore, be reformulated to: To what extent has the scope for the implementation of more outward looking strategies been already realized. It is not easy to give a clear-cut answer to this question because the different development paths of the almost heterogeneous Latin American economies in the sixties and seventies are superimposed by a number of more or less unsuccessful attempts to make an end to import substitution. Furthermore, numerous radical political changes limit the comparability of economic developments between the individual countries.

Despite these reservations, the evidence available of the policy experiences of the Southern Cone countries and Peru during the last 10-15 years will subsequently be used to grant support to some qualifying comments. The most ambitious liberalization (and reformation) efforts which have been undertaken in the Southern Cone after 1974, obviously failed to survive the world economic depression of the early eighties. A similarly negative result has to be registered in Peru, where the modest trade liberalization programme of 1981/82 broke down when the GDP growth rate dropped about 12 % within one year (1983) - partly due, however, to natural disasters.

There is a variety of literature on the courses of these failures (Canitrot, 1980; Edwards, 1985; Foxley, 1980; Nogués, 1985; Congdon, 1985; Herberger, 1985). While monetarists claim an inadequate application of their instructions (Sjaastad, 1983), structuralists believe that the instability of the capitalist system itself poses a fundamental limitation to liberal economic policies. However, apart from idelogical positions one can find a number of inherent inconsistencies of the economic strategies applied to these four countries which should be avoided in the future. For one thing, it appears to be nearly unquestionable now that binding the whole development process to one single monetary indicator (la tablita) clearly overstrains the adjustment flexibility of the market system. This is especially so, when fundamental institutional reforms are lagging (Argentina) and trade liberalization and financial reforms are counteracting with each other (Chile, Uruguay). Furthermore the transition from "import substitution" to an "export promotion strategy" implies an intersectoral transformation of real resources to the exportables sector. For national private entrepreneurs to follow such a policy advice willingly, the economic program must reflect a certain degree of reliability consistency and continuity of the new data. Taking in mind the historical experience with economic policies in many Latin American countries, and the instabilities during the transition period itself, the reversal of private investors's expectations becomes an especially important problem (see, for example, the case of Uruguay between 1974-78). Finally, in as much as trade reforms go hand in hand with a severe economic recession, export incentives will be picked up by any inefficient national producer, trying to minimize total loss out of existing capacities - but new investment will hardly take place in the export sector. In this case, which appears to be characteristic for Peru between 1975-80, surprisingly high export growth rates are rarely a proof for international competitive strength.

4. Latin American Economic Development and the Debt Crisis

In this last paragraph some concluding remarks are to be made on the national and international aspects of Latin American debt problems. It will be argued, that both sides, the participants in the international financial system as well as the Latin American countries, have to work on a cooperative solution of the debt problem to avoid a negative impact of the present financial situation on future prospects of developing and industrialized countries.

Firstly, it goes without saying, that economic recovery in Latin America will not be possible, as long as the severe macro-economic disequilibria are not corrected. Three digit inflation rates (Table 5) and extraordinarily high fiscal deficits are not at all a viable basis for investment and growth.

Secondly, macro-economic adjustment, although a necessary prerequisite to growth, is surely not a sufficient one. Rather it has to be accompanied by far-reaching changes in the national incentive systems of most Latin American economies.

Thirdly, transition from inward to outward looking strategies, especially when they are implemented after an extended period of protectionism is a most complicated and time-consuming task and it will probably not work without a prudent management of change.

Fourthly, significant intersectoral changes have to be initiated if the merits of international markets are to be exploited efficiently. This important policy objective is effectively hindered as long as national markets are shrinking and the flexibility of national factors of production is insufficient.

Looking at this catalogue reveals that the scope for policy improvement to be carried out by national policy makers in Latin America is not at all depleted. In as much as the implementation of promising policy reforms allows for a better use of the already existing productive means (there is a lot of relatively skilled labour available) this will also have a positive impact on international lenders, private investors and those Latin American residents, who fly from national capital markets under present conditions.

However, in as much as the existing debt burden limits essential imports and the (necessary) consolidation of fiscal deficits is left to national austerity policy, adjustment is hindered and stable growth will not resume within the foreseeable future. And this makes the Latin American debt problem an essentially international one. This debt trap may most certainly be characteristic for the situation in Bolivia and probably for Peru, but it is not so evident in the case of Brazil and Argentina (despite the fact that the sustainability of recent improvements of the economic situation is at least questionable).

In any case even the industrialized countries appear to become increasingly aware that additional international assistance to the larger debtor countries is urgently needed if a creeping crisis up to the nineties is to be avoided. Furthermore, in a world of rapidly increasing interdependence the public good character of the "international financial system" is gaining importance and may increasingly stimulate the will of the leading trading nations to intervene in potential areas of conflict.

However, there is a long way from recognition to action as far as changes of international institutional arrangements and cooperative actions are concerned. This could be most clearly observed in the discussion of the so-called Baker Plan (*Neue Zürcher Zeitung*, 10.10.85 and 31.10.85). It appears to be doubtful, therefore, that the developing countries' desire for additional external funds will match with reality in the near future. This makes the fact, that commercial banks are reluctant to extend new credits to LDCs above what has been called "involuntary lending" (Cline, 1985, 186), to a most pressing international financial problem. In fact, if private banks are unable to stick to their prominent role within the international financial system and new lenders are not in sight, the external financing of economic developing may remain far below traditional levels.

From a pragmatic point of view LDCs may be well advised to rely most heavily on their own domestic capacity to improve economic performance rather than hoping for substantially increasing international financial assistance. This holds even more true as one can expect that international commercial credits and other private capital inflows will increase as soon as the improvement of the national economic performance of any particular LDC increases its international creditworthiness.

Notes

1. There are some exceptions to this rule, namely if credits are used to improve food supply and this will effect the productivity of labour.
2. The Mexican peso appreciated by 22% in real terms between 1978 and 1981 (Balassa, 1985, 210).

References

Balassa, Bela, The Cambridge Group and the Developing Countries, *The World Economy*, 1985 (a), pp. 201-218.

Balassa, Bela, Exports, policy choices, and economic growth in developing countries after the 1973 oil shock, *Journal of Development Economics*, V. 18, No. 1, May-June 1985 (b), pp. 23-35.

Canitrot, Adolfo, Discipline as the central objective of economic policy: An essay on the economic programme of the Argentine government since 1976, *World Development*, Vol. 8, 1980, pp. 913-928.

Cline, William R., International Debt: From Crisis to Recovery?, *The American Economic Review*, Vol. 75, No. 2, May 1985, pp. 185-190

Congdon, T.G., *Economic Liberalism in the Cone of Latin America*, Trade Policy Research Centre, London 1985.

Cuddington, John T. and Smith, Gordon W., International Borrowing and Lending: What Have We Learned from Theory and Experience?, in Gordon W. Smith and John T. Cuddington (eds.), *International Debt and the Developing Countries*, The World Bank, Washington, D.C., March 1985, pp. 2-17.

Díaz-Alejandro, Carlos, Good-bye financial repression, hello financial crash, *Journal of Development Economics*, Vol. 19, No. 1/2, Sept-Oct. 1985, pp. 1-24.

Edwards, Sebastian, Stabilization with Liberalization: An Evaluation of Ten Years of Chile's Experiment with Free-Market Policies, 1973-1983, *Economic Development and Cultural Change*, Vol. 33, No. 2, Jan. 1985, pp 223-254.

Filatov, Victor S. and Mattione, Richard P., Latin America's Recovery from Debt Problems: An Assessment of Model-Based Projections, *Journal of Policy Modeling*, 7 (3) 1985, pp. 491-524.

Fishlow, Albert, Coping with the creeping crisis of debt, in: Miguel S. Wionczek and Luciano Tomassini (eds.), *Politics and Economics of External Debt Crisis, The Latin American Experience*, 1985 (a), pp. 97-144.

Fishlow, Albert, The State of Latin American Economics, in: Interamerican Development Bank, 1985 Report, 1985 (b), pp. 123-148.

Foxley, Alejandro, Towards a Free Market Economy, Chile 1974-1979, *Journal of Development Economics*, 10 (1982), pp. 3-29.

Gregorio, José de, Deuda externa, escenario económico externo y cuenta corriente en Chile: Perspectivas para el período 1985-90, CIEPLAN, Notas Técnicas N⁰. 68, Santiago de Chile, Marzo de 1985.

Harberger, Arnold C., Observations on the Chilean Economy, 1973- 1983, *Economic Development and Cultural Change*, Vol. 33, 3, April 1985, pp. 451-462.

Hesse, Helmut, Keppler, Horst und Preuße, Heinz Gert, Internationale Interdependenzen im weltwirtschaftlichen Entwicklungsprozeß, Arbeitsberichte des Ibero Amerika Instituts für Wirtschaftsforschung der Universität Göttingen, Heft 22, Göttingen 1985.

Kharas, Hami J., The Long-Run Creditworthiness of Developing Countries: Theory and Practice, *Quarterly Journal of Economics*, 99, Aug. 1984, pp. 415-440.

Marquez, Jaime, Foreign exchange constraints and growth possibilities in the LDCs, *Journal of Development Economics*, Vol. 19, No. 1/2, Sept.-Oct. 1985, pp. 39-57.

Mehdi Zaidi, Iqbal, Saving Investment, Fiscal Deficits, and the External Indebtedness of Developing Countries, *World Development*, Vol. 13, No. 5, May 1985, pp. 573-588.

Morgan, Guaranty Trust Company of New York, World Financial Markets, Sept./Oct. 1985.

Nogués, Julio J., Distortions, factor proportions and efficiency losses: Argentina in the Latin American scenario, *Weltwirtschaftliches Archiv*, Bd. 121, H. 2, 1985, pp. 280-303.

Notaro, Jorge, La política económica en el Uruguay 1968-1984, Montevideo 1984.

Schinke, Rolf, Verschuldung und Anpassung, Arbeitsberichte des Ibero Amerika Instituts für Wirtschaftsforschung der Universität Göttingen, Heft 23, Göttingen 1986, forthcoming.

Sjaastad, Larry A., Failure of Economic Liberalism in the Cone of Latin America, *The World Economy*, 6, March 1983, 1, pp. 5-26.

Wiesner, Eduardo, Latin American Debt: Lessons and Pending Issues, *The American Economic Review*, Vol. 75, No. 2, May 1985, pp. 191-195.

World Bank, Coping with External Debt in the 80s, An Abridged Version of World Debt Tables 1984-85 Edition, Washington 1985.

World Bank, World Development Report 1985, New York 1985.

World Bank, World Economic Outlook, April 1985, IMF, Washington 1985.

Mexico's External Debt and the Oil Question*

MIGUEL S. WIONCZEK

The full understanding of financial, economic and political implications of the Mexican external debt makes it necessary to look closely at the evolution of the Mexican debt spiral, both public *and* private between the early seventies and the early eighties, i.e. during the period in which the country's oil sector went through the full bust-boom-bust cycle. Moreover, one must analyse in detail the 1985 public sector external debt long-term rescheduling arrangement, considered by the Mexico's foreign creditors, the IMF and the U.S. Government as a model agreement to be followed by other large developing debtor countries whether in Latin America or elsewhere. The prospects for the eventual settlement of the Mexican debt in the light of deteriorating international oil market situation are discussed in the final part of the paper.

Undertaken in the aftermath of the deep domestic economic crisis started in 1982 and contrary to high expectations Mexico's efforts to put its economy in order through a dialogue with the international financial community about the ways and means of finding some workable solution for its external debt explosion brought very limited results. The first short and medium-term rescheduling arrangements of the public sector's foreign debt (due between 1982-1984) provided the point of departure for the rescheduling of more than 50 percent of the private sector's foreign debt. The second already mentioned long-term public sector's foreign debt rescheduling arrangement of 1985, involving 48,700 million dollars, most probably saved the country from the immediate bankruptcy. While this rescheduling has been hailed as the most complex of

* The author appreciates very generous assistance of Roberto Gutiérrez and Oscar Guzmán from Energy Research Program of El Colegio de México in the elaboration of this paper.

58

all carried out worldwide in the recent times and the first concluded by any major Latin American debtor country, only a few months after its entry into force there is no evidence that this jumbo financial operation involving the IMF, central banks of 42 creditor countries and 634 private institutional creditors assures Mexico both economic recovery and socio-political stability. It is left to the readers to find out in this rather long essay the answer to the question why all the "mountains" put together gave the birth to a far from impressive mouse.

I. Some Characteristics of the 1970s Foreign Debt Spiral

Although in Mexico the seventies are identified as the decade during which foreign indebtedness became a deliberate tool of economic development, the choice of this particular and in longer-term self-defeating approach goes back to the sixties and can be linked with the economic growth model, fashionable in other Latin American countries as well, known as that of *desarrollo estabilizador*. Its authors and practitioners argued that external debt offered one of the least inflationary development instruments, which could contribute largely to three important economic policy objectives: a high and sustained rate of economic growth, a low rate of inflation, and a coexistence with the then reigning internationally fixed exchange rate system. The achievement of these worthy objectives looked possible in a large developing resources-rich country at the time when international inflation was very low and the world economy and international trade kept growing at a fast pace. These favorable external conditions lasted unfortunately only during the first twenty five years of the post-war period. When they came rather abruptly to the end around 1970, the change was largely unnoticed anywhere in the so-called market economies. It is exactly around 1970 when Mexico's development model started running into trouble.

In the sixties the availability of foreign financial resources permitted Mexico to sustain a permanent deficit in its balance-of-payments current account and also to cover growing government deficits without inducing inflationary pressures by excessive domestic money creation. Since the inflow of external savings permitted the country also to abstain from such unpopular policy measures as a serious fiscal reform, it was both politically and economically very attractive. Moreover, the magnitude of this inflow was still rather reasonable compared with the size of the domestic economy and most of the foreign liabilities of Mexico took the form of long-maturity and low-interest credits granted by international official development banking institutions.

The predominance of the external official lending in the Mexico's foreign borrowing have already started to decline in the mid-sixties. As the Mexico's external capital needs continued to expand the trend towards switching to private financial intermediaries accelerated. By 1973, 55 percent of the public sector outstanding foreign debt was owed to private financial institutions and by 1976 this ratio had grown to 75 percent.

Until the mid-seventies things continued still under control. Although Mexico's public sector foreign debt kept growing steadily, its total as a percentage of gross domestic product (GDP) remained below 15 percent. Suddenly, in 1976, because of a host of domestic political, social and economic problems resulting in contraction of private investment, poor foreign sector performance, capital flight and the first peso devaluation after 22 years of fixed parity, the debt stock-GDP ratio jumped to 28.5 percent not to return ever to the levels of the previous decades. Although by the late seventies Mexico became a large oil exporter, the economy entered into a period of domestic economic instability complicated by the impact of serious and persistent international crisis still considered by orthodox economists from industrialized countries as a business cycle.

The combination of problems of internal and external origin was not managed properly particularly with the advent of the oil boom which was to take care of everything more or less automatically. As a consequence, public debt service burden passed from less than 45 percent annual average of the balance-of-payments current account in the first half of the seventies to almost two-thirds during the period 1976-1982 exceeding in some particular years 80 percent. By the same token, net annual public sector indebtedness went up from 0.72 percent of GDP in 1971 to 16.4 percent in 1975 and to 35.8 percent in 1982. In other words, by the early eighties Mexico fell into the "debt trap": new credits became necessary just to pay off short-term interest while the outstanding debt had to be rolled over. This emergency mechanism fell apart when (a) short-term debt had passed from less than 5 percent of public sector's total foreign debt during 1978-1980 to 17.5 percent during 1981-82; (b) the implicit interest rate on Mexico's public foreign debt had jumped up from just over 7 percent during the 1971-1979 period to more than 13 percent in the three following years; and (c) the exposure of some, particularly the US banks, had grown to a degree considered by lenders too risky without the changes in Mexico's economic policy. Additionally, since in the late seventies and the early eighties the rate of growth of the public sector foreign debt exceeded the nominal rate of interest by several points, both debt service ratios (i.e. as compared with merchandise exports and with current account revenue) tended to grow faster than desirable, and public sector debt management started getting out of control.[1]

During the period 1971-1982 public foreign indebtedness grew at an annual average rate of over 25 percent, more than twelve times in only 11 years. There is not a single explanation of this phenomenon. And since no one with the exception perhaps of the IMF claims to have simple answers and simple solutions for the present international debt quandary one can hardly understand the Mexico's debt accumulation problems without keeping in mind the complex interaction of many factors.

The Mexican public sector foreign debt explosion - as that of the US public sector for that matter - has many different roots, faces and implications both of international and domestic character. While some may be financial or economic others are political and even socio-psychological. The acceptance of such a complicated working hypothesis leads inevitably to the "structuralist" approach since it seems to offer the only way to look at the issue of Mexico's external indebtedness over time through the prism of the underlying interlinked but disjointed economic and non-economic structures. Moreover, if the above mentioned working hypothesis is correct, the prospects for resolving or even alleviating the external structural disequilibrium, complicated by many internal disequilibria wether in Mexico or in other developing or even developed countries through adjustment, stabilization and liberalization programs, i.e. balancing external and internal accounts, looks like a far from feasible task. What seems even more serious is that the sum of all orthodox national adjustment programs can hardly be expected to be the right medicine to get the world economy out of its present chaotic conditions and assure recovery and reasonably stable and sustained rates of growth for all parts of that highly interdependent global economy.

On the face of it, Mexico's public sector external debt problems may be considered first as the outcome of overborrowing on the extremely unfavorable terms since the mid-seventies; second, of the lack of optimality -to say the least- in the internal uses of borrowed resources; third, of the extreme and unfounded optimism in respect to the future of international oil markets, and fourth, of fast and easy profit maximization goals of international private banks. Once, however, the expressions "overborrowing", "lack of optimality", "extreme optimism" and "profit maximization goals" are concurrently used it is necessary to look into these issues in more detail.

Mexico's shift in the early seventies from borrowing in public development financing agencies to that in private banking sources coincided with a change in the economic development strategy followed by the country since the Second World War, known as "fast" industrialization through "easy" import substitution. The administration, which took office in December 1970, considered that previously unattended problems, i.e. income distribution patterns, rural areas backwardness, indigenous communities' marginality and the like had to be taken care of. Such a decision amounted to a radical economic policy change. The traditional "stabilization model" of the late fifties and the sixties gave way to a set of expansionary policies i.e. public expenditure-led growth model. Public spending was to achieve many goals at same time - economic growth, income redistribution, industrial promotion, petroleum sector expansion, and social modernization. Although the shortcomings of the model became obvious with the economic and financial crisis of 1976, the last year of the administration which opted six years earlier for the economic strategy change, the large oil discoveries of the mid-sixties made Mexico particularly attractive to foreign private lenders. With the appearance on the political scene of the new administration at the end of 1976, international credit flows from the world financial system to the Mexican Government and its agencies, both financial (development banks) and non-financial (commercial and productive entities, particu larly Pemex, the state petroleum monopoly) accelerated.[2] Together with rapidly expanding petroleum exports and revenue, external borrowing became the main economic policy instrument. Although, foreign borrowing helped for a while to promote one of the fastest economic growth periods of Mexico's history, it also made in the eyes of the policymakers unnecessary both long postponed fiscal reforms and the adjustment of an overvalued exchange rate. These two most serious policy omissions together with the steeply increased cost of external financial resources brought about in 1981/82 a new economic crisis much deeper than that of 1976. Since by 1982 Mexico became the second largest foreign debtor in the less developed world, this particular aspect the Mexico's new crisis attracted the attention of the outside world. The external debt issue represented, however, only a tip of an iceberg of the much more complicated Mexican economic and social misadventure.

While the earlier pages of this essay drew attention to overborrowing and lack of optimality in the internal uses of foreign resources as major factors of the Mexican crisis of 1982, yet some other factors have to be also mentioned; otherwise the seriousness of the 1982 economic crisis in Mexico can hardly be fully understood. The new model adopted in 1976 was only partly new. Its main policy goals - a fast rate of economic growth with emphasis on industrialization and employment creation were the same as those of the previous model. Its two major pillars were to be foreign borrowing and one single commodity (petroleum) exports, both highly uncertain factors. What disappeared from the 1976 model were social considerations; what was left from the 1970 model was public-expenditure led-growth.

The new model did not work for a number of complicated reasons:

First, the contradictions within the industrializing development model and the infatuation with the exchange rate stability excluded after each successive devaluation any other way than foreign borrowing to close gaps in the balance-of-payments current account and public finances.

Second, the implementation of any other set of external and domestic policies was highly constrained by both the geopolitical position of Mexico and its integration into the U.S. economy.

Third, until the "point of no-continuation" has been reached in respect to borrowing abroad the access to private foreign lenders involved much less apparent conditionality than borrowing from international development institutions, whose resources have already started declining in relative terms at the end of the sixties.

Fourth, despite serious reservations in many parts, the Mexican State dedicated its efforts to the expansion of the petroleum industry infrastructure and industrial growth. In terms of foreign exchange needs this was a quite expensive concept of economic development.

Fifth, in the absence of adequate employment opportunities in the increasingly capital intensive energy and manufacturing sectors, the pressure of the growing labor force concentrated on the service sector, which in the final analysis had to be equated with the State and the public sector.

Sixth, the extremely rapid demographic growth over four decades (1930-1970), around 3.5 percent each year, called for ever increasing public expenditure - both on investment and current account - since private savings albeit highly concentrated were largely misspent or misallocated, while private capital investment was conditioned by the public sector economic policy performance, particularly during 1971-1976 and in the 1981-82 crisis.

Seventh, the discovery of huge hydrocarbon resources in the mid-seventies created a sort of growth euphoria in the country and fostered persistent misallocation and waste of financial resources whose availability during the 1976-1982 administration seemed to have no limits. While some declarations about Mexico's growth performance, made at the highest political level around 1980, may sound *ex post* grotesque, the fast remains that GDP annual growth targets set during the late seventies and the early eighties at 8 percent or more were achieved at the cost of the 1981/82 crisis.[3]

As regards unlimited optimism and fast profit maximization goals of private foreign lenders to Mexico after the first oil-shock of 1973/74, they clearly reflected a lack of profitable investment opportunities in industrialized countries during the period in which international private financial institutions became flooded with the OPEC countries' surpluses. Mexico's public sector overborrowing would have not been possible if private foreign lenders had not considered providing it with funds as being not only highly profitable but also riskless. During the late seventies there were more potential lenders to Mexico than Mexican borrowers. Not only was the international financial press but also the later Mexican Treasury ministers were witnesses of such a phenomenon. The oversupply of credit made Mexico raise its participation in total Eurocredits granted to less developed countries from 6 percent in the early seventies to 11 percent by 1975. By 1977-1979 the country became the largest borrower on the Euromoney market.[4] As in the eyes of private foreign bankers Mexico was one of the most promising LDCs economies, they competed so fiercely for a share in Mexico's borrowing that loans were made with spreads over the LIBOR of less than 0.5 percent.[5] While direct bank credits earlier constituted the Mexico's usual borrowing instruments, in the late seventies syndicated Eurocurrency loans became the most popular way for the country to tap financial markets. As a consequence of the greater reliance on the Euromarket, Mexico's foreign public debt diversified with respect to the number of nationalities of lending institutions. While the U.S. participation in the total external public debt decreased from 46.6 percent in 1977 to 31.6 percent in 1983, that of Japan, for example, increased over the same period from 5.4 to 14.2 percent.

II. The 1982-1984 Foreign Public Debt Rescheduling Agreements

When the first signs of the risks of lending to Mexico were noted by the international banking community, it responded with increasing commission charges and the spreads over and above the prevailing by then record-high international interest rates. The borrowing-lending business with Mexico continued briskly until the moment when practically all foreign lenders became convinced that "business as usual with Mexico cannot go on indefinitely" and the point was reached when short of a miracle the country could not only keep its debt amortization schedules but found itself unable to service on time the outstanding external obligations as well.

The "point of no return" or rather "point of no continuation" was reached shortly afterwards in August 1982. Two rounds of most complicated, but more successful than elsewhere, renegotiations of the Mexico's public sector external debt (August and September 1983) preceded by the rather speedily extended facility agreement with the IMF, were helped by the fact that at that point not only financial relations between Mexico and private foreign lenders but the future of the whole shaky international financial system were at stake. The first renegotiation covering the roll-over of US $ 22.9 billion of short and medium-term debt due between 1982-1984 allowed the government to pay to its creditors during these years only US $ 3.7 billion, with the net postponement of US $ 19.2 billion for eight years with four years of grace. The floating interest rate was negotiated at $1\frac{7}{8}\%$ over the LIBOR or $1\frac{3}{4}\%$ over the U.S. prime rate. A once-for-all commission of 1 percent was charged for the operation.

The rescheduling operation was accompanied by "fresh money" from different sources: (a) a new US $ 5 billion loan with a six year maturity and three years of grace at a rate of $2\frac{1}{4}\%$ over the LIBOR or $2\frac{1}{8}\%$ over the U.S. prime rate with a $1\frac{1}{4}\%$ "front commission", was granted to the public sector by commercial banks; (b) a US $ 2 billion of bilateral export credits were granted by lending countries' official export-import banks; (c) US $ 4 billion were received through the extended facility agreement with the IMF (three years); (d) a US $ 1,850 million credit was received from the Bank for International Settlements in order to avoid Mexico's payments' suspension and cover also some essential imports; and (e) interbank credit lines of Mexican banks' branches and agencies abroad were reconfirmed at the existing levels.

This almost instant rescheduling of a short-term part of the Mexican public foreign debt had two major inconveniences for the debtor country. First of all, it continued to be short-termed. Total debt repayments including the rescheduled ones, would have been much higher by 1985 than those originally due and a similar trend would continue up to 1990. Second, overall payments (i.e. the total of annual payments for the whole period of 1982-1990) were larger after rescheduling than before by

US $ 11.7 billion. Although the increase in repayments reflected in large part new credits granted to Mexico in 1983 and 1984, it was also due to Mexico's agreement to pay higher than ever spreads and commissions for fresh credit, as well as to cover rescheduling charges. The harsh terms of the 1984 rescheduling package had somehow to be absorbed.

Thanks to Mexico's strict adherence in 1983 and 1984 to economic and financial performance targets, contained in the extended facility agreement with the IMF, Mexico managed in the spring of 1985 to conclude a new rescheduling program - the first of major Latin American debtors covering not only short-term but also long-term public debt.

III. 1985 Long-Term Debt Rescheduling Arrangements

As of mid-1985 out of seven major debtor countries in Latin America (Brazil, Mexico, Argentina, Venezuela, Chile, Peru and Colombia) which together according to the ECLA preliminary figures,[6] accounted at the end of 1984 for 89.5 percent of the total Latin American external debt (360.2 billion dollars) only *one* - Mexico - was able to reschedule more than two-thirds of its outstanding public sector principal repayments by up to 14 years, while two other countries -Argentina and Chile-made less spectacular rescheduling arrangements. In all remaining cases the debt renegotiations were bogged down either at the IMF or at private creditors level or with both amidst the growing evidence that the IMF for its part, and the international commercial banks as well were becoming even tougher with the debtors than immediately after the Latin American debt crisis had erupted in August 1982.

Since all foreign parties involved in the most recent Mexican debt renegotiations i.e. the IMF, central banks of creditor countries, international private bankers, and last but not least the U.S. administration, hail the 1985 agreement with Mexico as showing the correct way which other external debt-ridden countries in Latin America and elsewhere should (or must) follow, it may be worthwhile to look in some detail into the cause of Mexico's 1984/85 negotiations with international private lenders, which dragged on for more than a year.[7]

This last round of Mexican external debt renegotiations started shortly after the signature in late April 1984 by the Mexican Treasury and a group of about 500 international private banks of a $ 3.8 billion loan agreement expected to cover the country's financial needs for 1984. The loan was granted for 10 years, with four and a half years grace on the repayment of principal. It carried an interest rate of either $1\frac{1}{2}$ percentage points over the LIBOR or $1\frac{1}{8}$ points over the U.S. prime rate, interest rates lower and maturities longer than those accompanying a US $ 5 billion loan package that Mexico signed in 1983 with the same group of international commercial banks. In both negotiations the principal parties were the Mexican Treasury and the so-called 13-bank advisory group composed of all major foreign private lenders and led by one of the highest executive officers of the Citicorp, William Rhodes. In the wings stood the highest office holders of the IMF and the U.S. administration.

While, as it should have been expected, the details of the Mexican initial position at the start of the negotiations have never been made public, its main features were leaked to the international financial press by foreign bankers in the second half of July 1984, after the end of the first phase of negotiations had been suspended for several weeks for "further consultations". The major leaks originated in a meeting of some 80 European commercial banks, held in London to discuss and hopefully to approve the progress reached during negotiations between Mexico and the 13-banks advisory committee during the previous three months.

As reported by the *Financial Times* after the London meeting the Mexican Treasury originally proposed a 15-year rescheduling of its public sector debt due between the end of 1984 and 1990.[8] It also wanted to get an agreement to include some debt that had already been rescheduled once as well as the US $ 5 billion loan received in 1983. It was also seeking a commitment from creditor banks that they would make fresh loans available to Mexico if international interest rates rose. Finally, Mexico asked for a lower interest margin on the rescheduled debt to apply from January 1, 1985 and for the elimination of any rescheduling fee.

In spite of the fact that in all these respects Mexico followed the spirit of agreements in principle arrived at by the June 1984 summit meeting in London of the seven heads of states of major industrial countries (longer maturities, lower margins and multi-year agreements), considerable opposition was met among the European and presumably many U.S. banks - principally in respect to two points: a) the length of the rescheduling operation and b) reopening loan agreements made after the Mexican debt crisis arose in 1982. The first subject was of particular importance to both parties not only in financial but in political terms as well, since everybody was perfectly cognizant that the International Monetary Fund's adjustment program for Mexico was to expire at the end of 1985 and that, moreover, there was no doubt that Mexico was not at all prone to enter into the new one. From the Mexican viewpoint the timing of the whole rescheduling operation aimed at closing the deal with private creditors before the end of the agreement with the IMF and preferably even before the content of the third letter of intent covering 1985 was to be approved by the IMF. In neither case was Mexico able to achieve its objective.

After three weeks of the second-round intense negotiations with the 13-banks advisory committee the shape of the final rescheduling agreement surfaced at the end of August 1984 - again through leaks to the international financial press by some major creditors banks. While the *Financial Times* called it "an elaborate compromise",[9] *The Wall Street Journal* attributed a large part of that compromise to the personal weight of one of the major actors behind the scene, Federal Reserve Chairman Paul A. Volcker, who according to the same source "has been pushing since late 1983 to reward debtors that have successfully reigned in their economies".[10] As far as the creditor bankers were concerned they emphasized that the agreement "does contain the best terms as yet offered to a troubled debtor nation".[11]

The final clauses of the rescheduling agreement duly signed on March 29, 1985, call for:

a) the postponement of US $ 48.7 billion of principal payments falling due between 1985 and 1990 and repackaging them into loans maturing over a 14 years period, the last due in 1998 with interest payments included covering only the first year;

b) revising previous agreements covering about US $ 23 billion in principal payments originally due through 1984, lowering interest rates and granting longer maturities, and;

c) reopening and granting more favorable terms on a loan agreement for US $ 5 billion, signed in 1983.

Thus, creditor banks yielded both on maturities and interest rates and accepted also the elimination of a renegotiation fee. Consequently, a Mexico's public sector principal repayment profile over 1985-1998 changed very considerably and the overall payments of the period got smaller by 2,153 million dollars as compared to the payments due before rescheduling. This shows the better terms of negotiation of this arrangement as compared to the previous one (1982-1984).

Yet international commercial banks' concessions on maturities and interest rates were not granted free. Mexico gave up on the most important point of monitoring the behaviour of the economy after the expected demise of the present IMF adjustment program at the end of 1985 and in addition accepted a conditionality clause in respect to the "final" rescheduling dates for $ 23.6 billion of already rescheduled debt to be repackaged into a new loan in 1987 and 1988.* Monitoring itself involves the procedure calling Mexico to set out its "own" medium-term economic and financial targets in consultation with the IMF. As the IMF will presumably not be "lending money" to Mexico from 1986 on and hence it be legally unable to seek to impose its own conditions, the IMF will monitor only how Mexico lives up to its "self-imposed targets" through the regular review of its economy which it is obliged to make under Article 4 of its charter. A small detail may be mentioned here: while during the period of the IMF stabilization program, the reviews of the economy of its clients take place annually, the agreed "voluntary" reviews of the Mexico's performance will be conducted twice a year. According to international financial press reports, Mexico will let creditor banks see all or part of the IMF's normally confidential reports so that they will have regular access to a detailed review of the country's economy. The "compromise" formula is attractive to both parties: while creditors see it as a guarantee of Mexico's "proper behaviour", Mexico may look at it as a contingency clause.

It is important to notice that the rescheduling arrangement was signed in two rounds. The first, which involved 28.6 billion dollars, was concluded on March 29, 1985. The second, which involved 20.1 billion dollars, was concluded on August 29, 1985. This second rescheduling was quite important for Mexico, as it showed that after five months of the first long-term public sector foreign debt rescheduling arrangement the world financial community kept backing the economic program and financial behaviour of the Mexican government. In this way, Mexico became the first nation to conclude a multi-annual renegotiation of its public sector debt with the international financial community.

An interesting feature of Mexico's long-term public debt renegotiations is an agreement which would allow non-U.S. creditor banks to switch up to 50 percent of their dollar-denominated loans into their own currencies. Moreover, the non-U.S. banks wanting to convert into dollar loans denominated in other currencies would also be allowed to do so. Creditor banks would have to make their decisions within six months after the rescheduling agreement came into force.

The purpose of this limited intercurrency swap is to diversify the risk arising from the accumulation of the biggest part of the Mexican debt in US dollars. Swap transactions may be attractive to creditors if the US dollar exchange rate continues falling, and to Mexico because of large interest rate differentials in distinct capital markets. Calculations

---

* The second clause was abandoned by the creditors in the summer of 1985.

which appear in Table 1 show that this swapping should allow Mexico to save US $ 5,146.8 million during the whole period 1985-1998.

The task of drafting legal instruments for each of the 634 creditor banks, that would permit the entry into force of the agreement in principle announced in August 1984 took more time than expected for a host of reasons.[12] Parallel to this complicated operation Mexico was involved in two others: a) with the IMF on the terms of the third and final year of the adjustment program originally signed in November 1982, shortly after the country's financial crisis, and b) negotiations of a trade agreement with the U.S., the first in the whole postwar period and related to the application by the U.S. of countervailing duties to imports from Mexico. While on the surface no links seemed to exist between these three subjects, it can be hardly considered circumstantial that all were brought to fruition within four weeks time - between March 26 and April 29, 1985 - in spite of Mexico's earlier position that each issue deserved separate treatment on its merits and with its own timing.[13]

A rapid survey of the comments about the "Mexican debt problem", made in the U.S. financial circles at the time Mexico had sent to its creditors the first debt rescheduling proposal, provides strong circumstantial evidence that in these private circles, within the U.S. Government and in the IMF as well the treatment of Mexico's debt question were considered as part and parcel of the much larger package including trade and investment matters. These close linkages were aptly expressed in an article, published in *The Wall Street Journal* at the beginning of May 1984 by a vice president of Lehman Brothers Kuhn Loeb, Inc. and a former economist at the IMF. Attempting to answer an intriguing question about the ways by which Mexico could be led to economic recovery the author offered a concise four-point program:

Table 1. Estimates of the Mexican debt, EEC area (Million U.S. $.)

	1977	1978	1979	1980
United Kingdom	3,500.0	3,750.0	4,160.0	3,950.0
West Germany	1,550.0	2,020.0	2,450.0	3,200.0
France	700.0	1,525.0	1,725.0	2,250.0
Others	775.0	975.0	1,220.0	1,750.0
Total	6,525.0	8,270.0	9,550.0	11,150.0

Source: Secretaría de Hacienda y Crédito Público

First, the (Mexican) government must stick with its current program of eliminating
subsidies and bringing down barriers to foreign competition, forcing Mexican
business to become more competitive.

Second, maintaining realistic interest and exchange-rate levels must continue to be
a priority.

Third, the government must persuade foreign creditors to pump funds into
dynamic and commercially viable but often undercapitalized private business in
addition to sovereign lending programs. Joint ventures, co-financing with the World
Bank and other regional development banks, and a special risk capital fund would
help.

Fourth, Mexico should ease restrictions in foreign equity investment not only to
attract the badly needed new capital, but also to speed the transfer of technology.[14]

The implementation of such a program -its author admitted- would
not be easy at all since "until now success has been on the financial front
while the economy has contracted tremendously, and the private sector
has hesitated to undergo the structural adjustments necessary to respond to new policies".[15]

The snowballing of the external debt and the debt service left aside,
the IMF adjustment program targets were not met because they could
not have been fulfilled without the deepening of domestic social tensions
beyond tolerable levels. Two particular IMF targets became the subject
of the long wrangle between the Mexican Government and the IMF: the
public sector deficit and the inflation rates.

The public sector deficit which as late as in 1982 exceeded 18 percent
of the GDP was more than halved in 1983 to 8.5 percent and was
compressed again in 1984 to 7.5 of the GDP, against the IMF target of
5.1 percent agreed by Mexico for that year in the previous letter of intent.
The over-shooting of the 1984 target was largely attributed to high
domestic interest rates, caused partly in that year by higher than expected inflation, which according to official Mexican figures was down
from 80.8 percent in 1983 to 59.2 percent but missed the mutually agreed
1984 target of 40 percent. The 1985 negotiations lasted almost three
months instead of several weeks which took the parties to agree the year
earlier. The 1985 agreement reflects an accounting compromise on the
deficit, originated partly on both sides from using different methods to
calculate it and partly from a cut in its overall size. According to
Washington sources the IMF toughness in late 1984 and early 1985 was
meant to provide indirect signals for other Latin American debtor
countries like Argentina and Brazil that do not meet the IMF performance targets.

IV. The Future of the Mexican Debt

At the time this essay is written (fall of 1985) whether Mexico will reach in 1985 the IMF targets for the public sector deficit and inflation rates seems a very secondary question. While official data are not available in Mexico or elsewhere in respect to the real social impact of the 1981-82 economic and financial crisis and the IMF supported adjustment program of 1983-84, there is more than circumstantial evidence to the effect that the income distribution pattern in Mexico and the real wages of the salaried people which represent about one half of the working force had already started deteriorating in the early seventies and continued to do so through the mid-eighties. It is estimated that between January 1981 and January 1985 the real wages of the salaried workers and lower public sector personnel were cut by 32 percent in real terms. While the rate of unemployment continues to be miraculously low (about 6 percent), some 40 percent of the urban working force falls into the category of under-employed. Under such social conditions food subsidies which account for the sizable part of the public expenditure just cannot be eliminated although constant efforts are made by the Government side to compress them under the IMF guidance. One of the "minor" points which held up the signing of the debt rescheduling agreement was foreign creditor banks' insistence of the abandonment of preferential interest rates on the Government credits to CONASUPO - the State-owned distributor of staple foodstuffs - (the point which creditors finally won). This detail indicates how little the international banking community understands and cares about Mexico's internal structural and political problems.

There was in the summer of 1985 a sort of general agreement in the country, although practically nothing can be heard along these lines in official circles and local mass-media except in the left-wing newspapers devoid of any political influence, that with the three parallel arrangements (the 1985 agreement with the IMF on the conditions of the last year of the adjustment program, the rescheduling of the US 48.7 billion of the outstanding public debt and the bilateral trade with the U.S.) Mexico has been just buying some breathing space for the short and medium-term. Whether these arrangements will create the correct frame of reference for the country's full and sustained recovery in the remaining twelve years of the present century is another matter, subject to which very few foreign and domestic official analysts of the Mexican scene dedicate much attention. *Ceteris paribus* the medium-term chances of Mexico's exit from the present crisis are not at all negligible and perhaps better than those of the rest of the region. But the *ceteris paribus* clause contains such a long list of external conditions to be fulfilled and domestic structural problems to be resolved, that it is completely impossible to project the behaviour of the Mexican economy between 1985 and 2000 and to indulge in speculation about its future. Moreover, two major disasters befell Mexico in the fall of 1985: the acceleration of decline in international oil prices and the serious earthquake in central Mexico with damages estimated at several billion dollars.

While the 1983-1985 tough adjustment was reasonably successful because of the earlier oil boom and the concurrent disorderly and costly build-up of the country's industrial structure, left idle in 1981-82, Mexico should be in a position over the next few years to service its external debt and somewhat diversify exports. But the potential available in this respect might be nullified almost overnight by the breakdown of international oil prices, the fall of the dollar and the subsequent extension of protectionist measures in the industrial countries. Furthermore, everybody in Mexico is aware that to get out of the present rot the country will need fresh savings. The answer to the question where these savings will come from is not available as yet. An approach to the Mexican holders of some 15 to 30 billion dollar assets abroad to bring money home seems to be difficult in the extreme. No case is known anywhere in Latin America as yet of the return of exported "private savings" and Mexico will not be exception to the rule whatever incentives the Mexican Government can offer to past sinners. After all, they were as much responsible for the Mexican financial and economic crisis of 1981-82 as foreign creditors charging extortionate interest rates on their loans and the domestic mismanagers of the economy at the public and the private level.

Although the need to increase the rate of "new" domestic savings is generally recognized no such phenomenon can occur under the conditions of a still rampant internal inflation. Since high inflation reflects political, social and economic structural problems it can hardly be dealt with by fiscal and monetary policy measures even assuming that some more coherent mix of such policies could be designed and implemented. The steadily deteriorating income distribution patterns, built into the IMF stabilization program, will continue to be fed by whatever policy measures and targets will take its place under the "benign surveillance" of the Mexican economy by the coalition of the IMF experts and foreign creditors after January 1, 1986. The wishing away of the income distribution deterioration is a very doubtful proposition at the time when the country's domestic shrinking market represents one of the major obstacles to development while external markets do not show any signs of expansion.

In the fall of 1984 some statements were made by the Mexican financial authorities to the effect that since Mexico will need in addition to the rescheduling of its public debt close to US $ 20 billion in the 1985-90 period, it was considering a market shift in its borrowing strategy by reducing its reliance on commercial bank loans notwithstanding the fact that already in 1985 the country hoped to regain uncontrolled access to the international capital markets.[16] After the debt rescheduling negotiations the emphasis was to be put on such sources as multilateral financial institutions, among them the World Bank, government export credit agendies and supplier credits. Anyone cognizant of the present capital shortage at the World Bank and the Inter-American Development ment Bank, the budgetary difficulties of government export credit agencies, including U.S. Export-Import Bank, and the general hostility of all the major industrial countries' governments to any initiative suggesting the liberalization of multilateral and bilateral export-supporting lending does not bode well for the Mexican plans for a new "external finance strategy" if the above quoted statements were more than rhetorical exercises.

Following this type of dispassionate analysis one sees that even if sometime later during the present decade Mexico reaches the elusive goal of domestic financial stabilization, it will be faced with the need for foreign private investment whose massive presence in the country during the last turbulent years instead of being helpful to the alleviation of the economic crisis was one of its aggravating factors. That foreign - mainly U.S. private investors - come (back) to Mexico seems to be assured. But the details of the negotiations of the U.S. - Mexico bilateral trade treaty in the spring of 1985 which transpired to the international financial press indicate that the political and financial costs of these new inflows of foreign private capital will be rather on the high side.

What is important now, some economic and financial circles insist, is how to make the debt rescheduling arrangement to stick through 1998 under the hopeful assumption that the international economic conditions will improve somewhat in the medium term. The course of these events is clearly beyond the control of Mexico and the developing countries as a group, although the constant pressure at the IMF-World Bank level and in other international forums, including the United Nations agencies may be of some help. Little is expected in real terms, however, from all these colateral multilateral political activities. In other words, each debtor country must face its tribulations on its own.

Within this frame of mind it is hard to find in the Mexican official circles much enthusiasm in respect to the feasibility of a wide range of operative proposals for the handling of the international debt issue, offered by all sorts of academic financial experts from both the industrial and the developing countries. What seems to worry the Mexican policy makers more than anything else is the issue of high real interest rates and their impact on the debt servicing burden after the 1985 rescheduling agreement. A technical paper, elaborated at the Center for Economic Studies of El Colegio de México as early as in December 1983, put this issue in very clear terms:

> There is a clear trade-off between the rate of interest and the rate of growth of output. The persistent unorthodox economic policy of the United States, characterized by a large public deficit, does not show a very bright perspective for the future of interest rates. The burden of the debt will not be substantially reduced in the near future, and thus the rates of growth of the Mexican economy cannot be expected to recover their historical tendency, unless there are drastic changes in the current institutional arrangements...
>
> The foreign debt in Mexico has reached levels that, even under optimistic scenarios, impose foreign exchange requirements that can be met by the economy only if substantial costs are incurred. Mexico cannot have low rates of output growth for a sustained period of time while retaining political stability.
>
> Non-oil exports might be able to grow at high rates, but it will be very difficult to sustain them. Only if the interest rates are substantially reduced and/or institutional arrangements suffer a drastic change, will Mexico be able to realistically service its debt in the long run.[17]

The question what should be done if the international interest rates are not abated within a reasonable time was analysed at length by a Mexico's Central Bank official in charge of reorganizing the private sector's external debt, Ernesto Zedillo de León in April 1985. While sustaining the position that in the case of Mexico and other Latin American countries "adjustment had to take place irrespective of the IMF's intervention", Zedillo de León added in a not particularly diplomatic language that:

> Quite paradoxically, the contribution of other important official lenders - either multilateral or bilateral - to the solution of the debt problem has been quite modest, if not detrimental in certain cases. That is not to say that reschedulings of liabilities owed to official entities were totally absent from the picture. The trouble was (and still is) that, in general, official creditors - when not openly rejecting restructuring - have frequently pursued and reached better terms than those obtained by private creditors. A supposedly firm intention to continue lending, and even increase exposures, has constituted the main argument provided by official creditors for not matching the schemes negotiated with the private banks. In assessing this position, it should be considered, however, that it is not the same to commit resources as to

effectively provide them. Many inflexibilities of a legal and economic nature may be built into the credits thus arranged, and preclude their use, even if the need for foreign savings is enormous.[18]

Furthermore, Zedillo de León sounded quite pessimistic in his evaluation of future trends of the real interest rates in international capital markets, adding that the combination of high interest rates and a constantly appreciating dollar make it very difficult for developing countries to prevent the substantial outflows of private capital that clearly bring about enormous complications for the debt problem.

If conditions such as the control of the U.S. fiscal deficit, a greater monetary policy coordination among developed countries, and the reversal of the new protectionism, are not to be accomplished in the foreseeable future - the Mexican central banking expert continued - the time might be ripe to go ahead on the debt front with less orthodox albeit rational and responsible schemes. Among them he found particularly appealing the Brazilian proposal of worldwide income-tax-free bonds issued by LDCs' debtors, and the capitalization of interest payments exceeding certain reasonable ceilings.[19]

The lessons of the most recent Mexican long-term debt rescheduling operation for the rest of the LDCs and in particular Latin American debtor countries are rather clear. They may be presented in the form of a list, which far from being all inclusive, attempts to highlight the key issues involved:

　　a)　the international "debt bomb" is going to tick for some time yet;

　　b)　the renegotiation of external debt is a political, economic and financial power game between very unequal partners whether individually or groupwise;

　　c)　as the issue is not only about money lent by creditor countries but about the whole system of relations between the industrial market economy countries and the LDCs; in that respect a recent statement of an ECLA economist to the effect that "the increase in the cost of the debt as a result of the renegotiations is nothing but a monopoly rent which is extracted from the (debtor) countries by virtue of the emergence of a non-competitive capital market" is only partially correct;[20] while in the case of Mexican renegotiations maturities were extended, interest rate differentials slightly cut and "front commissions" foregone, other ways were found by creditors to countervail their small and quantifiable concessions by the Mexican counter-concessions under the umbrella of the "benign and informal" surveillance to be managed discretely by the

IMF from now to almost eternity and supported by the clauses of the U.S.-Mexican bilateral trade treaty; and

d) below the surface of polite official statements from creditor countries that there is the commonality of interest between creditors and debtors in search for a just and working solution, the longer-term debt renegotiations are a very rough game; the skills and the abilities of the Mexican negotiators were equal to those of their foreign counterparts, but what was unequal was the respective power position; what creditors, fully supported by their governments, were aiming at was the maximization of gains of all sorts in the long run whereas a debtor country, in this case Mexico, wanted only to minimize losses.

Viewed from the creditor countries' viewpoint the "special treatment" offered to Mexico during the 1984/85 rescheduling debt renegotiations paid apparently large short-term political dividends: the initiatives with respect to the common Latin American debtors' action, immediately and incorrectly dubbed by the creditors as a "debtor cartel", whose possible emergence became for the industrial north in 1982 and 1983 a short-time nightmare, lost their appeal to the region; in the light of the Mexican long-term arrangement - the creditor countries thought - multilateral negotiations would be forgotten; every debtor country will also understand that if it behaves, shows "understanding" of the creditors' position and accepts the rules of the game, it may receive also some preferential treatment; otherwise a debtor country will be left to its own devices and will face a very uncertain future.

Unexpectedly, the Mexican debt story did not end in mid-1985. Shortly afterwards, it became clear at least in Mexico itself that the chances for the implementation of the latest grandiose rescheduling arrangement were not particularly good due to the steady deterioration of the international economy, on the one hand, and to the increasing domestic political and social costs, on the other. Only in the light of this growing uncertainty in Mexico with respect to the longer-term viability of the rescheduling agreement, one can understand several calls by the Mexican finance minister deeply involved in its having been put together for "fresh money" and a statement made by Mexico's President, Miguel de la Madrid in an interview granted to *The Wall Street Journal* in mid-September whose parts related to the debt question read as follows:

What Mexico is seeking, is the creation of an international awareness so that the necessary cooperation mechanisms may be established for the benefit of all and a new debt crisis may be prevented because every crisis would surely be greater... There is a growing awareness among the creditor banks, which are concerned that their credit portfolios might suddenly have to suffer considerably; but also among the central banks, because they would surely have to come to the rescue of their own banking systems, and that, in turn, would have an impact on their countries' general economies.[21]

Moreover, things are becoming complicated on other Latin American fronts. Brazil made it clear that it was neither ready nor willing to follow the Mexico's "model" debt rescheduling agreement; Fidel Castro of Cuba made considerable political capital from his persistent calls to many Latin American dissenters asking for the repudiation of the whole region's indebtedness, and the new President of Peru, Alan Garcia chose the day of his inauguration in August to declare unilaterally that his country will service its external debt to the extent of 10 percent of Peruvian exports revenue. All these most recent developments strongly suggest that the issue of external foreign indebtedness is far from being settled both in Latin America and in Mexico itself. Even some highly conservative economists from the fringe of the present U.S. Administration seem to be coming around to the idea that the repayment of the Latin American debt at any cost to the debtor countries is an unrealistic dream of the creditors. It may seem both highly unusual and somewhat strange to read in *The Wall Street Journal* these days quotes from an article published some time ago in Stanford University's *Campus Report* by Prof. Robert Wesson, head of Latin American Studies at the impeccably conservative Hoover Institution, to the effect that:

> The old loans made for unproductive purposes cannot be repaid, short of debt slavery unacceptable in the modern world. They should be recognized as unpayable and cancelled... The wisest course would be for the U.S. to negotiate a write-off... The U.S. cannot prosper all on its own, ignoring the plight of its clients and customers... obviously, all the banks will have to agree on a concerted plan. It will be useless for the U.S. to agree to a moratorium or cancellation of the debts if the Europeans won't go along.[22]

V. The Mexican Oil Question and the Debt

One might expect that the large scale oil and natural gas discoveries of the mid-sixties and the country's forceful entry a few years later into international crude markets would alleviate considerably the external indebtedness burden. For the purpose of understanding why it did not happen a brief excursion into the field of financial policies followed between 1970 and 1985 by the Mexican oil sector, run by the State enterprise PEMEX, may be in order. Following the patterns adopted at that time for the public financing as a whole, external credits and, in particular, foreign capital goods and services suppliers became since the mid-sixties a major source of financing for the oil sector. Reasons for its growing dependence upon external financing were rather simple: while the rapid expansion of demand for energy of all sorts called for the concurrent growth of hydrocarbon supplies, PEMEX was starved of its own savings for close to two decades because of the energy price policy which kept real petroleum products domestic prices falling down. Moreover, the absence of fiscal policy reforms made the oil industry's access to the Federal financing more and more difficult. Finally, domestic private savings, however misallocated, concentrated in the manufacturing and service sectors.[23] Consequently, out of about US $ 4,800 million invested by PEMEX between 1971 and 1976 no more than US $ 500 million came from domestic sources (net profits, if any; open and disguised Federal subsidies, and proceeds from the bonds sales to the public). The remaining US $ 4,300 million were borrowed abroad.

Consequently, while the liabilities of the oil industry increased between 1970 and 1976 three and a half times during the period of a still relative domestic price stability, its net foreign liabilities grew fivefold to some US $ 2,800 million by the end of 1976. The acceleration of the rhythm of foreign indebtedness could have hardly been avoided since domestic oil products demand overtook supply between 1970 and 1974, making Mexico during this period a net crude and products importer. Growing activities in exploration, crude production and processing capacity paid rather handsome dividends in balance-of-payments on current account. By 1975 Mexico not only stopped spending foreign exchange on oil imports but it had established the bases for the oil boom of 1978-1982. The structure of the PEMEX external debt showed, however, serious weaknesses.

With the oil industry switching progressively from international multinational agencies and suppliers' credits to international private banks almost one half of its liabilities took the form of short-term loans in spite of the obvious fact that the maturing of projects in the oil industry normally exceeds five years. Not only did foreign credits have on average rather short maturity but interest rates were inexplicably higher than those paid on the credits obtained by the rest of the public sector. Thus, although in the light of large crude discoveries the short-run PEMEX financial position was by the end of the 1970-1976 administration still solid, looking at it *ex post* one can see the harbingers of the difficulties ahead.

With the emergence of Mexico as a large potential oil exporter shortly after the change of administration in late 1976, oil was declared the pillar of an accelerated economic growth and modernization. The further expansion of hydrocarbons productive capacity and the creation of crude export-oriented infrastructure involved large and rapid investment needs. In the light of the continued policy of depressed domestic oil products prices, the PEMEX dependence upon external financial resources increased once again. Between 1977 and 1979 revenue accounted by foreign credits reached one third of the oil industry total revenue and its outstanding debt reached at the end of 1979 close to US $ 10 billion, more than three times than that owed at the end of 1976. The external debt service burden grew proportionally even more because of the increase in international interest rates and the persistence of the earlier observed preference for short-term credits obtained now almost exclusively from international private financial intermediaries. But apparently the situation was under control since the PEMEX debt was still at the end of 1979 below the industry's foreign exchange revenue estimated for the following year at about US $ 10 billion.

If the proceeds from foreign financial sources would have been reasonably allocated no debt servicing problem would have emerged within a number of years. That resources allocation was very far from perfect it is another story. Consequently, real problems emerged as early as in 1980 as the consequence of the continued and accelerated PEMEX borrowing in the face of the growing instability of the international capital market and persistently high interest rates.

In spite of the disappearence from the political seene in 1981 PEMEX Director General Jorge Díaz Serrano, the chief architect of the Mexican oil-led growth strategy, almost unlimited oil industry borrowing continued. The external liabilities grew during the three-year "boom" (1980-1982) period at the average annual rate of 35 percent of the industry's revenue and the actual volume of debt transactions increased 5.4 times in comparison with the indebtedness rate of 1977-1979 to the first half of the 1977-1982 administration. A large part of "fresh money" was used to repay some earlier short-term debts and service the outstanding PE-MEX indebtedness as suggested by the fact that while the new net PEMEX borrowing in the 1977-1982 period amounted to about US $ 16,000 million, the total debt stood at the end of 1982 at US $ 25,200 million as compared with little below US $ 3,500 million six years earlier.

As no detailed data are available on actual uses of money borrowed abroad between 1977 and 1982 and, particularly, on the value of PE-MEX physical investment during the same period, the magnitudes mentioned above, first, suggest that the cost of almost permanent PEMEX debt "rescheduling operation" must have been extremely high and, second, explain foreign bankers' unlimited willingness to lend to the Mexican oil industry and the industry's management eagerness to borrow almost until the very day of national reckoning in the fall of 1982. Without attempting to estimate even *grosso modo* "leakages" that occurred on both sides of the oil industry - international financial community borrowing-lending fence under the Mexican oil boom conditions, one is prone to come to the conclusion that its management by the two parties directly involved represented a very considerable contribution to Mexico's post-1982 woes and difficulties of all sorts.

This negative contribution was only partly compensated by PEMEX considerable effort from 1983 on to bring its debt problems under control by reducing its external contractual liabilities (close to 80 percent of its total external debt) from US $ 19,700 million to US $ 16,500 million or by US $ 2,700 million, and renegotiating some of its credit lines in the U.S. and Great Britain for two more years. Moreover, the PEMEX debt has apparently not been included in the 1985 rescheduling arrangement of the Mexico's public debt to the amount of US $ 48.7 billion, discussed at length earlier. It may be recalled just for the record that the total oil industry debt, which stood at the end of 1982 at US $ 25.2 billion was composed of US $ 5 billion equivalent of domestic liabilities and US $ 20.2 billion of external debt and its maturities were divided almost equally between short-term and long-term.[24]

The question which remains to be answered in this part of the essay is whether the present PEMEX debt is manageable. The experience of the oil industry between the end of 1982 and the spring of 1985 would strongly suggest a positive answer to this question if PEMEX liabilities could be considered in isolation from Mexico's global financial and economic problems. Mexico's record as a crude producer and exporter and the supplier of domestic market in energy imputs for the 1980-1984 period has been reasonably satisfactory, despite the difficulties caused by the weakening world oil prices and the falling levels of energy demand in the industrialized countries. PEMEX investment plans for the 1983-1988 administration period reflect both international oil market instability and the decline of domestic energy demand in the wake of the August 1982 crisis. Moreover, most recent studies of energy savings and conservation potential in Mexico offer convincing and detailed evidence that there is a very large margin in this respect in the Mexican oil and gas industry.[25] Assuming also the impact of steep increases in oil products prices on domestic demand, one may assume that during the next several years, PEMEX will be able to keep its production at the levels reached on the eve of 1982 except in exploration and natural gas domestic distribution sectors. The total volume of investment in the oil and gas sector is within the reach of PEMEX financial possibilities particularly if the degree of internal waste is somewhat reduced. Thus, in principle PEMEX's future seems to be assured.

This encouraging statement, however, must be qualified on two accounts, both largely outside of Mexico's control. First, PEMEX at the present stage carries not only a manageable burden of its indebtedness but that of the whole of Mexico. In other more explicit language in the absence of PEMEX Mexico would have gone bankrupt in 1982. Pemex net export revenues kept at an almost even keel during 1983 and 1984 when compared with Mexico's record revenue from crude oil products exports in 1982 (US $ 16 billion), permitting to support successive debt restructuration arrangements. More than 70 percent of the oil industry foreign exchange revenues were dedicated to servicing the country's outstanding debt.[26] Since the fall of 1985 PEMEX financial capability is in doubt because of the breakdown of the extremely fragile equilibrium of the international oil market after Saudi Arabia's walkout for all practical purposes from the OPEC councils. Mexico's foreign exchange revenues will most probably fall in 1985 by US $ 2 billion largely because of a decline in crude export prices. While in the short-run, this shortfall may be compensated by "savings" in the debt service due to the debt rescheduling agreements, under no circumstances could the Mexican economy survive the collapse of international oil prices to below US $ 20 a barrel, expected by many and feared by even more actors in the international oil trade game.

As far as the overall links between the Mexican short lasting oil boom of 1977-1982 and the external debt accumulation and its explosion in 1982 are concerned they should be clear to the patient readers of this essay. Without the oil boom the debt explosion would have been postponed in Mexico for a while only but not forever. The strategy of basing the long-term growth of the Mexican economy upon foreign borrowing and petroleum was unworkable all the way through. In a way it confirmed the validity of an answer allegedly given around 1980 by a finance minister of a Middle East country to a question: How does one feel running a country in which all financial constraints suddenly disappear? The answer was: under such conditions all other constraints are felt more than ever.

The participation of the EEC member countries in the Mexico's external debt has been growing steadily over the past 10 years. The total Community member countries' exposure increased between 1977 and 1984 from US $ 6,525 million to US $ 18,815 million and in each of both years accounted for slightly over 28% of the Mexican external debt. The EEC credits consist in part of direct loans by individual, particularly British, European banks and in part of participations in the 1983-85 period.

It is understood that in the light of the limited exposure of European banks in Mexico they adopt much more relaxed attitudes vis-à-vis the country's external debt problems than the U.S. banking community. Their position seems to be shared by a number of governments of the EEC countries. Both West European Government and Bankers believe that in a longer-term Mexico will "muddle through" and get out of its present external debt predicament.

As far as the short and medium-term prospects are concerned there is consensus in Mexico itself to the effect that the successful "muddling through" wil depend to quite an extent not only on internal policy efforts but on the degree of cooperation of the creditor countries both at official and private banking levels on both sides of the Atlantic. The purpose of this essay is not to dramatize Mexico's external debt difficulties but to provide European readers with an analysis of their magnitude which calls for a new concerted approach on an international scale that would permit the country both the economic recovery and growth and the escape from the "debt trap".

Notes

1. For a quantitative analysis on Mexico's debt problems see Ortiz, Guillermo and Jaime Serra Puche, "A Note on the Burden of the Mexican Foreign Debt" Centro de Estudios Económicos, documentos de trabajo No. 1984/II, El Colegio de México, December 1983.
2. Pemex foreign debt during the 1970s grew impressively. See Gutiérrez R. Roberto, "La balanza petrolera de México, 1970-1982", in *Comercio Exterior*, vol. 29, No. 8, August 1979, particularly Table 8 and pp. 842-843. It is important to stress that Pemex foreign debt participation in that of the public sector passed from 10.3 percent in 1970 to about one third in 1982.
3. Wionczek, Miguel S., "Industrialization, Foreign Capital and Technology Transfer - The Mexican Experiences, 1930-1985". Paper presented at International Seminar on Growth Experience in India, Brazil and Mexico, New Delhi, April 1981, (mimeo), pp. 20-21.
4. Green, Rosario, "México: Crisis financiera y deuda externa", Seminario sobre la Economía Mexicana - Situación Actual y Perspectivas Macroeconómicas, El Colegio de México, Mexico, August 1983, p. 7.
5. *Ibid.*
6. ECLA/CEPAL, *Balance preliminar de la economía latinoamericana durante 1984*, LC/6. 1336, December 24, 1984, Santiago de Chile, (mimeo).

7. In the light of scarcity of information available in Mixico outside of official communiqués and speeches most of this reconstruction is based on reports of international financial press covering March 1984 - August 1985 period. The U.S. "rescue operation" of Mexico in the fall of 1982 is described and analyzed in Kraft, Joseph, *The Mexican Rescue*, Group of Thirty, New York, 1984.

8. Montagnon, Peter, "Mexican Debt Plan Given Cool Response", *Financial Times* (London), August 6, 1984.

9. Monagnon, Peter, "Mexico to pay at least $ 1 billion of Principal", *Financial Times*, September 10, 1984.

10. Witcher, Karene S., "Banks Give Ground on Mexico Debt Terms in Exchange for Close Watch on Economy", *The Wall Street Journal*, (New York) August 30, 1984.

11. *Ibid.*

12. Montagnon, Peter, "Debt rescheduling - Mexico's push settingway forward", *Financial Times*, September 12, 1984.

13. Not all small creditor banks subscribed to the Mexican debt rescheduling deal and there are reports from London about a volume of transactions in secondary markets with Latin American debt instruments at discount, which in the case of Mexico is about 20 percent, the lowest in the region.

14. Bogdanowich-Bindert, Christine A., "Getting Mexico from Remedy to Recovery", *The Wall Street Jounal*, May 2, 1984.

15. *Ibid.*

16. "Mexico to request $ 20 billion in 6 years", *Financial Times*, September 14, 1984, quoting an official document presenting to creditor banks Mexico's financial objectives and leaked by London banking sources.

17. Ortiz, Guillermo and Jaime Serra Puche, *op.cit.* pp. 25-26.

18. Zedillo Ponce de León, Ernesto, "contribución a la mesa redonda sobre la problemática del endeudamiento externo de América Latina", Va. Convención Bancaria de Panamá, Panamá, April 1985, (mimeo), p. 6.

19. *Ibid.* p. 20.

20. Devlin, Robert, "The Renegotiation of the Latin American Debt", *ECLA Review* No. 20, 1984, Santiago de Chile.

21. "De la Madrid at the Halfway Mark", *The Wall Street Journal*, September 10, 1985.

22. Quoted in Cockburn, Alexander, "Heed the SOS on Third World Finances ", *The Wall Street Journal*, September 12, 1985.

23. For details see Guzmán, Oscar, *Finanzas de la industria petrolera mexicana (1970-1985)*, Programa de Energéticos, El Colegio de México (in press).

24. *Ibid.*

25. Guzmán, Oscar, Antonio Yúnez-Naude and Miguel S. Wionczek, *Energy Savings and Conservations in Mexico: Experiences and Prospects*, Westview Press, Boulder, Col. (in press).

26. Wionczek, Miguel S., "Mexico's Hydrocarbon Industry Performance and Prospects" *OPEC Review*, Vol. IX, No. 2, summer 1985, Vienna, pp. 141-147.

PART 3
INDUSTRIAL POLICY

Industrial Policy in Mexico: Problems, Objectives, and Relationship to the EEC

SAÚL TREJO REYES

The analysis of Mexico's industrial policy and the possible ways in which the country's future development relates to the European Economic Community must be placed in a broader context, that of the relationship between Mexico's industrial policy, on the one hand, and the country's national objectives and the international environment it faces, on the other hand. As one of the so-called newly industrializing countries (NICs), Mexico has received a great deal of attention, but especially so beginning in the late seventies, as newly discovered oil wealth made the country a natural magnet for all kinds of commercial enterprises from developed countries.

Despite the oil bonanza and the more recent foreign debt crisis, the problems facing industrial policy over the long run have remained more of less constant. Among these, it is to these kinds of issues that we shall address ourselves in this paper. The first part of the analysis deals in a general way with the broad context of current Latin American economic development. The second part briefly describes the country's industrial development and structure over the last forty years, and the third part presents a brief analysis of Mexico's trade with the EEC, the structure and rate of growth of manufacturing output, the productivity of industry, the country's ability to generate sufficient foreign exchange to meet development objectives and the relationship between industrial output and employment growth are among the most important. The fourth part presents the challenges facing Mexican industrial policy at present and in the foreseeable future, exploring some of the possible avenues for further economic cooperation between Mexico and the EEC. Finally, a brief section deals with the relationship between inflation and industrial policy in the Mexican context.

Like most developing countries with a high foreign debt, Mexico faces a number of difficult choices with regard to industrial policy. Basically, it must transform its economic structure, and particularly its industrial sector, in order to become attuned to the new world economic and technological realities. This means that, in order to generate the trade surplus needed to service the foreign debt, the country must become an efficient producer of the kinds of goods demanded by modern industrial countries. It must do so while at the same time it must try to fill a number of unmet social needs, the greatest of which is for adequately paid jobs for its growing labour force. In some ways, the decisions that the policy-makers must make are perhaps no more difficult than in the past; however, there is a greater number of complex elements that must be taken into account, so that the mere extra-polation of past trends no longer constitutes an adequate basis for industrial development policy, as was often thought in the past. At the same time, and to a much greater degree than in European countries, the need to maintain a certain degree of political consensus represents an important restriction to the set of policy alternatives available.

Common Problems for Latin American Countries

During the foreseeable future, most Latin American countries, and especially Mexico, will face very difficult economic and social problems as a result of some basic structural characteristics. First, they must try to meet the demand for new jobs resulting from a young and growing labour force whose needs and expectations can only be met, as a necessary but not sufficient condition, by a high rate of growth of national products. Such an objective is thus of primary importance for Mexico's policy-makers. At the same time, however, the country's large foreign debt represents a key restriction to economic growth, since debt service payments by the government, which are a rather high percentage of government expenditure, reduce the amount of resources available for development. Besides, the large absolute size of the country's foreign debt means that an active fiscal policy can hardly be used to achieve higher growth rates; it would be very difficult to finance the resulting foreign exchange deficits under current circumstances.

The net result of this double "crunch" between growing social needs and shrinking economic possibilities is that Latin American countries face the need to make much greater structural adjustments than European countries. Perhaps some of the adjustments Mexico must make are greater than those facing other countries in the region; however, the difference is one of degree only. It should be pointed out that in most of Latin America, the absolute levels of per capita income, as well as its highly unequal distribution, lend great urgency to the problems of employment creation and satisfaction of the basic needs of the population.

Table 1 presents the growth of both population and the labour force beginning in 1940. As may be infered, employment creation requirements during the next few decades will be particularly high. There are a number of problems with the 1980 Population Census and the labour force figure for that year is most likely overstated; however, the upward trend from the past decade is unmistakeable. Despite the relative success achieved by population policies,[1] this will not be reflected in lower growth rates for working age population until the mid-nineties. In fact, the number of persons annually reaching working age will keep on increasing right through to the end of the next decade. Only then will it reach a plateau and gradually begin to fall.

With regard to foreign debt, the basic data are shown in Table 2. As may be seen, from 1974 on the ratio of foreign debt to GNP has grown constantly. Per capita debt has also increased substantially during the period, as have debt service and the debt service ratio. Thus, for the foreseeable future and despite the recent renegotiation of the debt, service payments will place a heavy burden on the country's import capacity. As a result, one of the main objectives of the country's industrial policy must be to increase import capacity and to raise the efficiency of imports. Otherwise, it simply will not be possible to achieve

Table 1. Mexico: Population and Labour Force, 1940-1980 (Millions)

Year	Population[1]	Annual growth rates	Labour force[2]	Annual growth rates
1940	19,654	—	5,858	—
1950	25,791	2.8	8,272	3.5
1960	34,923	3.1	11,253	3.1
1970	48,225	3.3	14,430[3]	2.5
1980	66,847	3.3	22,066	4.3

1. *Population Censuses*, various years (Dirección General de Estadística, *Censo General de Población*, 1940,1950,1960,1970,1980, México, D.F.).
2. *Population Censuses*, various years.
3. Wivan Ginneken, *Socio-Economic Groups and Income Distribution in Mexico*, (London, Croom Helm, 1980), pp. 94-95.

the rates of growth that are required to maintain social stability, given the high rates of population and labour force growth.

The third basic problem that industrial policy must face in Mexico is how to orient industrial sector development towards a greater degree of satisfaction of the populations's basic needs. Given the highly unequal distribution of income, and the high rate of growth of population, one of the main areas of growth for the industrial sector must no doubt be the satisfaction of basic consumer goods demand. However, this not only requires that the country be able to generate the required foreign exchange to pay for intermediate goods imports; at the same time, the kinds of goods the industrial sector produces must be affordable for the majority of the population. This means not only producing certain kinds of goods, but also achieving a high level of productive efficiency, in order to have a reasonable level of internal prices.

As may be seen, in the main aspects, Mexico's economic problems are in general similar to those of the rest of Latin America. However, given the size of its population and the degree of industrialization already reached, its future growth depends much more on its being able to compete

Table 2. Mexico's foreign debt and debt service

Year.	Public foreign debt[1]	Public foreign debt service/GNP percent	Per capita foreign debt[2]	Debt service ratio[3]
1974	9 975	1.8	175	18.5
1975	14 449	2.4	246	29.6
1976	19 600	3.1	323	33.7
1977	22 912	4.3	366	38.8
1978	22 264	6.1	345	54.0
1979	29 757	7.6	448	63.1
1980	33 813	4.1	494	30.7
1981	52 961	4.3	753	33.9
1982	58 874	6.0	816	35.0
1983	62 556	6.0	845	30.0

1. Millions of current dollars
2. Current dollars. Refers to public debt only
3. Ratio of public debt service payments to export receipts, in percentage points. For 1970-1981, the source is *10 años de Indicado res Económicos y Sociales de México*, Secretaría de Programación y Presupuesto (México, 1983). For 1982 and 1983, it is *Segundo Informe de Gobierno de Miguel de la Madrid, 1984*, (México, 1984), Sector Política Económica, p. 846.

successfully in international markets in order to pay for its import requirements.

Mexico's Industrial Structure and Development

The period of intensive industrialization in Mexico began with World War II. Before this time, manufacturing's relative importance was rather low; in 1940, it accounted for 18 percent of GNP, measured in 1950 pesos.[2] Under a mix of protectionist policies, industrial output grew rapidly beginning in the early forties. First as a result of import shortages caused by the war, and later as a result of explicit policy decisions, import substitution became an engine of growth. Throughout this early period of industrialization, industrial output grew considerably faster than GNP; by 1960, manufacturing's share had risen to 23 percent.[3] By 1980, it was up to nearly 25 percent of GNP.[4]

As in practically all developing countries that began to industrialize in the immediate postwar period, production of consumer goods with a high import content was the first stage in this process. However, unlike other newly industrializing countries, recent growth in Mexico has been in general higher in consumer goods output; at the same time, the country's reliance on imported capital goods has also remained high. As a result of a policy bias in favour of consumer goods production, and of the fact that the newer industries have in general had higher import requirements, the import elasticity of output growth has remained rather high. In 1970-1981 its average value was 1.16. At the same time, the country has lagged behind other NICs in its ability to increase manufactured goods exports.

As a result of the failure of manufactured goods exports to rise sufficiently fast, industrial growth has been accompanied by a tendency to growing balance of trade deficits. Beginning in the mid-fifties, such deficits were financed by foreign credits and direct foreign investment. Even though the relative importance of such deficits has grown through time, up until the early seventies they were not a matter of great concern to policy makers. It was generally thought that they would disappear in time as a natural result of economic growth. However, throughout the sixties, there was a growing realization of the need to transform industrial development policies in order to make exports more attractive. In spite of this realization, little was done in the way of changing basic development policies. Thus, throughout the postwar period, protection from import of manufactures has remained rather high, both through the use of tariffs and of an import licensing system. This has tended to favour industry vis-à-vis the rest of the economy, especially the primary sector.

As a result of a policy of favouring industry, through protection from foreign competition, through favourable prices of industrial inputs produced by public sector enterprises or by government, and through large government investments in industrial infrastructure, manufacturing output grew rapidly for most of the period through 1981. Efficiency levels have been far below those prevailing in industry in developed countries; at the same time, however, rates of return on invested capital have remained generally high. By and large, government policies to favour industry have not included technological development of productivity growth as objectives. As a result, most Mexican firms have remained highly dependent on foreign technology and capital goods; at the same time, they have consistently opposed domestic growth of such activities, fearing the limit they would eventually place on their access to foreign technology, capital goods and inputs.

The country's reliance on imported technology and capital goods is of course, directly responsible for the high import elasticity of output growth. At the same time, lack of a vigorous technological base and capital goods sector contributes directly to a growing absolute balance of trade deficit. This tendency was aggravated during the oil boom period, 1978 to 1981; to the limit size of the capital goods sector were added the effects of rapid growth on the demand for capital goods and of an increasingly overvalued exchange rate, which made imports of all kinds, including consumer goods, considerably more attractive.

While in general the types of industrial development policies followed during the last decades don't differ greatly from those adopted by many Latin American countries, the acceleration of technological progress and the rapid diffusion of knowledge, which are now global phenomena, have meant a growing pressure to import new kinds of consumer goods, to adopt new production processes and to invest in new types of capital goods. Imports of such goods and services have remained highly profitable, given the height of tariff and non-tariff barriers. However, by and large development and adaptation of new technologies has not been deemed to be an attractive use of private resources; even in the absence of such activities, profit rates in industry have remained high. At the same time, efforts by government have been too few and too dispersed with regard to stated policy objectives in order to make an impact at the level of the firm. As a result of the technological lag that such behaviour has implied, insofar as national producers are hardly ever in on the first, and most profitable, stages of the product cycle, exporting has never been a really attractive activity. By the time Mexican products reach foreign markets, competition is keen and prices have fallen below new product introduction levels. Just the opposite conditions prevail in the domestic market; a high rate of protection has kept prices of industrial goods far above world levels.

Mexico's Trade with the EEC

Mexico's foreign trade pattern has historically shown a great similarity to those of other developing countries; exports of primary products have traditionally accounted for the bulk of exports. Manufactured goods exports have tended to be made up of traditional, simpler types of manufactures. The rapid increase of oil exports after 1978 and the resulting economic boom emphasized the traditional pattern of exports; as the exchange rate became increasingly overvalued and Mexican products lost international competitiveness, only resource-based or traditional manufactured goods continued to be exported, besides agricultural and mineral products.

Within this context, Mexico's trade with the EEC is easily understood. The country has traditionally run large deficits in its trade with EEC

Table 3. Mexico's trade with the EEC 1975-1984 (Thousands of Dollars)

Year	Total[1]	Exports		Imports[1]	Balance[1]
		Non-oil (percent)	Oil		
1975	263 954	100.0	0.0	1 061 552	−797 598
1976	298 185	100.0	0.0	949 103	−650 918
1977	272 113	100.0	0.0	846 683	−574 570
1978	341 867	100.0	0.0	1 489 770	−1 147 903
1979	521 180	99.7[2]	0.3	2 152 930	−1 631 750
1980	1 134 473	56.8[2]	43.2	2 556 712	−1 422 239
1981	1 647 686	35.1[2]	64.9	3 247 154	−1 599 468
1982	2 618 865	24.8[2]	75.2	2 223 235	395 630
1983	2 273 882	26.7[2]	73.3	1 189 895	1 083 987
1984	2 610 524	18.1[1]	81.9	1 351 043	1 259 483

1. Secretaría de Programación y Presupuesto, Mexico. Unofficial Data.
2. Eurostat, E.E.C., Quoted in unpublished study by the Mexican commercial attaché, Rotterdam.

last few years, as a result of oil exports, that the net balance has been favourable to Mexico. However, given that practically one hundred percent of oil export receipts must now be used to service outstanding foreign debt, the country still faces a serious disequilibrium in its economic relationship with the EEC.

The composition of trade between Mexico and the EEC shows that the main exports to the EEC are at present crude oil, honey, zinc concentrates, cotton, sulphur, automobiles and typewriters. In 1984, oil accounted for 82 percent of Mexican exports to the EEC, a proportion even higher than in total Mexican exports, where it was approximately 75 percent of the total. By contrast, automobiles accounted for 2.2 percent of the total and typewriters for only 0.8 percent. All other exports are in general of a traditional nature. Manufacturing exports in 1983 accounted for only 10.3 percent of the total.

Mexican imports from the EEC, on the other hand, have been considerably more advanced. Again, in 1983, manufactures accounted for 99.4 percent of Mexican imports from the EEC. The main types of products imported from EEC countries were metal-working machinery, iron and steel pipes, locomotives, metal products, machinery of all types, industrial compounds and sea going vessels. Three countries, Germany, France and the United Kingdom accounted for 89 percent of Mexican exports to the community and 75 percent of imports.

As may be seen, trade between Mexico and the EEC falls very much within the traditional pattern of North-South, or developed countries - developing countries trade. From the point of view of Mexico, future increases in economic cooperation between the country and the EEC will only be possible in a new context that takes into acount mutual interests as well as the changes in world trading patterns that may be expected in the future.

Challenges for Industrial Policy

As had been pointed out, the industrial sector has played a rather limited role in solving the main problems facing the country, among them the balace of payments deficit. In fact, as has been pointed out, the import requirements of industrial expansion account for a large part of total imports. Were past tendencies to continue, industrial growth would not be able to break out of the deadlock imposed by insufficient foreign exchange earnings. Thus, perhaps the main objective of current industrial policy is to overcome the sector's adverse balance of trade, and this countries, both individually and taken together. It has only been in the means achieving a high rate of growth of manufacturing exports. The economic crisis the country has faced since 1982 has rendered obsolete the arguments that have been traditionally used by manufacturing firms to explain their failure to export, and that various groups had considered as valid. The main arguments used by industry have been, up until early 1982, the overvalued exchange rate, and the "incipient" and inefficient nature of domestic industry. The latter argument has been considerably emphasized in recent discussions about future commercial policy, by opponents of trade liberalization.

In the period since 1982, of course, the exchange rate has been devalued by well over 1000 percent. However, non-oil exports rose considerably only in 1983, more as a result of depressed internal demand than of a permanent increase in the country's export capacity. It is evident, then, that the inability to export is not exclusively an exchange rate problem, as was often argued in the past. Insufficient technological development and unsuitability of products for world markets are definitely the more serious problems except perhaps for traditional or primary exports.

Given that increasing exports drastically is an essential national objective, it follows that higher efficiency levels should be a first priority for Mexican industry. Thus, government policies toward industry must change drastically during the next few years if such objectives are to be reached. The current Administration has set out to implement such changes, although it has met strong opposition from several groups. A high level of efficiency necessarily implies a much higher level of integration to the international economy, not only in terms of the higher level of exports the country must achieve, but also with regard to the volume and kinds of imports which will be essential to attain higher levels of productivity in industry. Greater integration to the world economy will be by no means an easy task, given the size of the trade deficit for industrial goods and the lack of technological capacity on the part of most of Mexican industry. However, there is no other alternative which will, at the same time, produce the foreign exchange needed for industrial growth and allow a sufficiently high rate of employment creation in manufacturing. On the other hand, the country must of necessity be very conscious of the need to maintain control of its own economic policies, essential if it is to avoid the pitfalls of becoming simply a source of cheap labor and raw materials for multinationals.

The need to transform Mexican industry into a net exporting sector in the short, or at least in the medium run, has a number of important implications. First of all, it implies the need to modernize Mexican industrial firms, which traditionally have been only oriented to satisfy domestic demand; they have lacked a market orientation and the capacity to modify their products in order to compete in different types of markets. And this is perhaps one of the areas where the country must look for a greater degree of cooperation and trade with modern firms from industrially advanced countries. What's needed and what the country is seeking, however, is not to further the traditional foreign investment type of scheme, which in the past has simply meant that foreign firms have looked at the country primarily as a market for components, to be assembled locally if that humours the host, or as a market in which it must establish a presence simply to avoid giving it up entirely to competitors. Given the country's present and future foreign exchange deficit, the only way in which foreign firms can contribute to the country's long term objectives and at the same time assure the long run feasibility of their own investments is to produce a favourable balance of foreign exchange for the country. This will only be possible if both foreign investors and the government are able to go beyond their traditional views with regard to the role and criteria for successful foreign ventures. At the same time, a dynamic industrial sector will only be a viable objective if the country's heavy and inefficient distribution system is significantly improved, in order to reduce commercial margins, so that industrial firms can be profitable while at the same time lowering prices to final consumers.

Thirdly, the growing imbalance between the structure and growth patterns of demand, on the one hand, and the structure of industrial productive capacity, on the other, also implies a need for the country to participate more actively in world trade - otherwise it would be increasingly expensive to try to perform satisfactorily. Past import substitution policies have been primarily oriented to satisfying domestic demand; however, as a result of the rapidly accelerating pace of economic and technological change in the industrially advanced countries, such a policy is increasingly unviable for Mexico. Simply put, there are too many products to make and the structure of demand is to diversified for any but the largest country to adopt a policy of autarchy. At the same time, as a result of technological advances in transport and communications, a world market is a reality for an increasing number of products; large firms must attempt to compete on a world scale in order to be effiecient producers, and this places a growing pressure on inefficicent, domestically-oriented firms in any country.

It may be argued that in a country such as Mexico, the structure of demand does not change as rapidly as in developed countries; however, the impulse in that direction is unmistakable. As a result, the rate of obsolescence in industry has increased substantially over time; this represents a definite disadvantage for firms with a lower level of technological sophistication since they are less able to adapt to such rapid changes. Such firms now have a shorter period of time to master new technologies, which they have usually acquired from abroad. At the same time, exporting is now a much more difficult goal to attain for such types of firms, given the much higher level of efficiency and innovative capacity required to make exporting of manufactures a profitable activity.

A salient aspect in explaining the evolution of demand for manufactured products in Mexico is the growth of the middle and upper class. As a result of such growth and of increasingly faster communications, a growing percentage of the population shows a pattern of demand for consumer goods which resembles ever more those characteristic of developed countries. Such a phenomenon not only raises the demand for consumer goods imports but, given past protectionist policies, has created ample investment opportunities based on producing limited volumes of output at prices far superior to those prevailing in other countries. This has diverted resources away from sectors or activities with a higher export potential but which are, under protectionest policies, not as profitable as import substituting sectors.

During the next few years, one of the main goals of industrial policy must be to change drastically the product mix of industry, in order to increase the relative importance of intermediate and capital goods in total output. At the same time, industrial policy must explicitly take account of the changes in the cost structure of industrial production over the last few years in the more advanced countries. In such structures, direct production costs have a rapidly decreasing relative importance; at the same time, "indirect" activities, such as research and development, product design and engineering, marketing and other "information-based" activities account for a growing percentage of total production costs. Given the country's weakness in these stages of the productive process, which happen to be the best paid, and which also have a multiplier effect on new firm creation, during the next few years industrial policy must face the challenge of increasing the relative importance of such types of activities in industrial firms. In the past, both domestic and foreign firms have tended to "import" such elements, since they have been generally neglected by protectionist policies. However, the country's export goals cannot be met unless such behaviour is drastically changed.

During the foreseeable future, the nature and speed of technological change on a world level will continue to be such that, rightly, the process is characterized as a new industrial revolution. Progress in areas such as electronics and its application to production processes, to communications and to all kinds of intellectual activity - biotechnology and new materials - most clearly foreshadows a radical transformation of the nature of industrial activity, of relative prices of products and factors of production, of trade flows and of many other areas. In such a context, Mexico's industrial policy must consider the need for choosing and channeling new investments accordingly. To do otherwise implies running the risk of being stuck with an increasingly obsolete structure of production capacity and with a price level for industrial output which would make it all but impossible for Mexican manufactures to compete internationally.

It should also be recognized in formulating industrial policy in countries such as Mexico that technological change, and especially the application of new technologies to traditional industries, is in many cases "rejuvenating" such ageing sectors. This is no doubt slowing down, and even reversing, what only a few years ago was considered an almost certain "redeployment" of traditional industries to developing countries, in search of cheaper labour, energy and natural resources. While such a process has occurred in some cases, there is no doubt that modernization in ageing industries, as well as strategic and internal political factors in advanced countries, have held back industrial redeployment and considerably limited its scope for the foreseeable future and its potential for generating income and export growth in developing countries.

It is in this context that Mexico must take a substantial effort during the next few years to attract and/or develop high-tech industries, with favourable potential. Evidently, attracting or developing high-tech industries in the country and having them effectively become strong exporters is a goal that can only be reached in gradual stages. In the first stage, it is essential that exporting firms in "desirable" or priority industries be given ample facilities to import parts, components and equipment. At the same time, the government has already recognized the need to make an intensive effort to simplify and reduce bureaucratic procedures. It is also essential that this process of redirecting industrial investment be accompanied by serious efforts to identify and develop opportunities for increasing the domestic content of industrial production, but without making this a rigid requirement. Otherwise, costs would rise and industrial products would lose international competitiveness. What must be a key element right from the initial operating of new investments is to achieve a net positive foreign exchange balance. This should always be possible, from the very first stages, for new projects with a majority of foreign capital.

Inflation and Industrial Policy

The high rates of inflation that Mexico has experienced beginning in 1973, and especially after 1982, have made it very difficult to plan industrial development in a rational manner. The real exchange rate has varied widely over the period; at times it has been highly overvalued; on the other hand, after the succesive devaluations it has tended to be undervalued. (See Table 4). Such fluctuations have meant rather wide variations in the degree of real protection accorded to different types of industrial goods over time.

Table 4. Exchange rate in Mexico 1970-1984

Year	Nominal[1] rate	Prices[2] US/Mexico	Real rate	Real rate (index)
1970	12.50	100.0	12.50	100.0
1971	12.50	99.3	12.41	99.3
1972	12.50	97.3	12.16	97.3
1973	12.50	91.3	11.41	91.4
1974	12.50	81.5	10.19	81.5
1975	12.50	77.2	9.65	77.2
1976	15.41	68.0	10.48	83.8
1977	22.58	55.2	12.46	99.7
1978	22.77	50.7	11.54	92.4
1979	22.80	45.9	10.47	83.7
1980	22.96	37.8	8.68	69.4
1981	24.51	31.5	7.72	61.7
1982	57.44	20.8	11.95	95.6
1983	120.17	11.2	13.46	107.7
1984	169.59	7.0	11.85	94.8

1. Average for the year. After 1982, the controlled rate is used. The free market rate has varied more widely and has been between 20 and 30 percent above the former. *Segundo Informe de Gobierno de Miguel de la Madrid*, (México, 1984)
2. Banco de México, *Informe Anual, 1984* and *Economic Report of the President*, U.S. Government Printing Office.

Secondly, and also a result of the high rates of inflation, relative prices different types of products have varied rather widely over time. Among the factors that have contributed to this growing dispersion, one may cite the differential rates of growth of supply and demand, differences in tariff rates for various kinds of products, price control policies and different rates of technological change in the production of different types of products, market structures, and so on. As a result, in part, of the changing pattern of relative prices, a number of unwanted effects, from the point of view of policy objectives, have followed. Among these are the higher profitability of sectors such as commerce and those that produce luxury consumer goods, and the depressed rates of return in production of basic consumer in capital goods.

At the same time, a number of important distortions in the behaviour of firms have ensued as a result of the high rates of inflation and the failure of various policies to fully take account of the phenomenon. Fiscal policies have traditionally considered the cost of assets as the basis for depreciation allowances, while treating nominal interest costs as fully deductible from taxable income. As a result of such policies, during an inflationary period fiscal depreciation understates economic depreciation and thus causes taxable income to be considerably overstated. On the other hand, the full deductibility nominal interest payments in effect implies being able to deduct from taxable income what is in fact a prepayment of debt. This of course tends to benefit more highly leveraged firms, which in general are the larger firms in Mexico. Thus, fiscal and financial policies have, by default, become very important elements of industrial policy. This unintended result has important implications for future policy-making; unless these policies are brought into line with industrial development objectives, it would appear to be rather difficult to achieve stated policy objectives in this sector.

This management of pricing policies also becomes vitally important during an inflationary period. Traditionally, price controls and parallel subsidy schemes have been important policy instruments in Mexico. Not only have price controls and subsidies been used to achieve resource allocation objectives; the main stated purpose has been to try to keep down price increases, primarily for basic consumer goods. Given the objectives of economic efficiency and high rates of growth of productivity, relative price policies are an area of particular importance for industrial policy, since relative prices are an important signal for channeling savings flows to different sectors. This not only refers to investment financed directly by business firms but, more importantly, to resources allocated through financial intermediaries.

Concluding Comments

During the next few years, Mexico's industrial policy must gradually evolve toward a much greater degree of flexibility, in order to adapt a rapidly changing international environment. Doubtless, this will present a number of interesting possibilities for achieving a higher degree of complementarity with advanced industrial countries, among them those of the EEC. Naturally, a key objective of Mexico's industrial development strategy must be the rapid increase of non-petroleum exports, in order to relieve the country's foreign exchange constraint. In order to achieve such a goal, new industrial investments, by both Mexican and foreign firms, must contribute directly to the development of a highly efficient productive structure, fully able to compete in international markets and to lower the domestic price level through greater competition. Evidently, the task of transforming the structure of national output to make Mexican goods more competitive in foreign markets opens ample possibilities for different types of cooperation with modern firms in advanced countries.

Notes

1. The rate of growth of population has fallen from 3.5 percent annually in 1970 to 2.2 percent in 1984, according to the latest estimates.
2. C.W. Reynolds, *The Mexican Economy: Twentieth Century Structure and Growth*, (New Haven Yale University Press, 1970) pp. 60-61.
3. Ibid.
4. Measured at 1970 prices. *Anuario Estadístico de los Estados Unidos Mexicanos, 1984.* (México, Secretaría de Programación y Presupuesto, 1985), pp. 443.

The Industrial Policy of the European Communities: Between Cooperation and Competition

ELISABETH DE GHELLINCK

Industrial policy is a matter of quite recent concern for governments. The aim of industrial policy is to create optimal conditions to enable structural changes to be carried out. An examination of the Rome treaty reveals that industrial policy is completely absent. The creation of a unified open internal market was thougt to be enough to reach the general socio-objectives as laid down in article 2, namely the promotion of economic expansion, growth of employment and a rising standard of living. Access to an enlarged market would enable the firms to achieve economies of scale and hence increase their productivity, whilst at the same time confrontation with producers from other countries would increase competition, drive prices down and favour innovation. In this way, the process of industrial adjustment is automatically and continuously realized by a decentralized competitive system. The main instruments of such an implicit market-oriented industrial policy, following the abolition of internal tariffs, were those designed to assure the Common Market, namely competition policy, a common external policy and authority to favour harmonization of member state laws.

The unprecedented period of growth of the 50s and the 60s favoured openness and cooperative economic relationships which were felt to increase national as well as world welfare. Despite the fact that the establishment of the internal market and the liberalization of world trade were eased by this propitious environment, the crisis of the seventies revealed the inability of European industries to adapt to new internal and external constraints.

Before discussing the actual contents of the European industrial policy, we want to show that the dismantling of the internal barriers has not provided a sufficient impetus to help European firms to face a competitive world. Natural barriers but mainly strategic barriers - to entry or to exit - erected by firms in order to maintain their dominance or by governments in order to protect national interests are such that several markets remain imperfectly competitive; in such a context, there is no guarantee anymore that the market mechanism rationalisation operates efficiently. Growing scepticism about the virtues of the competitive adjustment process developed.

At the end of the transition period, in 1970, the Commisssion observed that despite the fact that the dismantling of internal tariff barriers had been a great success, only industries serving the private consumer benefited from the customs unions whereas industries exploiting new technologies failed to break out of the frontiers of each national market, dependent as they were for their development on public funds and orders. Furthermore, the impact of integration on the structure of firms or on the growth of industries was judged insufficient.[1]

Using its power of recommendation the Commission asserted clearly and publicly the necessity of defining a common industrial policy, with the aim to allow industry to derive the maximum advantages from the existence and size of the Common Market and to stimulate the dynamism of the market. Following the Commission, the completion of the internal market entailed the removal of technical barriers to trade, free access to public contracts, establishment of a concerted public procurement policy and elimination of tax frontiers within the Community. As regards the second objective, various measures which would favour the adjustment of industrial structures were proposed: promotion of new technologies through a science and technology policy, monitoring of structure of production through the competition policy, adjustment of the conditions of trade through the commercial policy and adaptation of the infrastructure through a common transport and energy policy.

The Commission insisted on the fact that the action of the Community is to organize, to make consistent and hence more effective action to be taken at national or even at regional level. However, specific concerted action at the Community level was felt necessary for declining industries whose adaptation has to be foreseen and eased and progressive industries whose development is conditional on a propitious environment. Along these lines, the Commission suggested the promotion of European transnational firms in sectors where size is thought to be a prerequisite for an arms-length competitive process in international markets. To ensure that the expected increase in concentration is not attained at the expense of competition, a merger control is proposed as from 1973. At the external level, the Commission insisted on an extented solidarity among member states to other fields than tariffs, such as investments and technology. In the absence of a political consensus, these propositions were rejected or watered down by the Council.

During the seventies, Europe faced major challenges: the rise in the price of raw materials, the expansion of new competitors (the NICs) into its traditional export markets - steel, shipbuilding, textiles - and the increasing competitiveness from Japan and the US in the field of advanced technology. The inability of European industrial structures to adapt rapidly and smoothly to this new environment revealed a lack of industrial dynamism. As Geroski and Jacquemin (1985b) argue, part of the explanation lies in the policy aimed at creating European super-firms large enough to compete with the American ones which resulted in a huge merger wave and the constitution of big national champions sheltered from market forces.[2]

As recession and unemployment replaced expansion, the evolution of the European Community became characterized by intense internal tensions and strong solidarity. On the one hand, it was no more evident for Member States confronted by the problem of overcapacity that national and community interests coincide.[3] As protection of national industry allows a country to slow down the pace of structural adjustment and to export unemployment problems, Member States were induced to react in a defensive and inward-looking manner by means of aids and national regulations in the field of technical standards. On the other hand, the deepening of the crisis made a more cooperative attitude more necessary. At the external level, Member States became aware of the fact that the negotiating power of the Community in international trade is greater than their individual power and hence that any action to improve the terms of trade is much more efficient when taken at the Community level. At the internal level, interdependence[4] among Member States is so high that national protectionist measures become inefficient and harmful as they are mutually destructive.[5]

In this context of commercial struggle, the market does not necessarily select the most efficient firms but those which benefit most from financial resources - be they public or private. This is particularly evident in the case of declining industries. In the field of new technology, strategic behaviour on the part of both governments and firms is an important feature of certain imperfectly competitive high technology industries. Artificial barriers to trade and natural barriers linked with the financial investment needed and the economics associated with learning from longer production runs are such that the viability of a new firm in these markets depends on a guaranteed access to European or even to world markets. This implies a commitment of European governments to support these projects; this commitment will be efficient if it is credible, i.e. if it affects the decision of firms to enter these markets.[6] The effort made by the Airbus consortium to compete with Boeing in the market for intermediate-range commercial jets is the best known instance[7] of such strategic behaviour. Hence, as shown by Dixit and Kyle (1985), subsidies could be attractive[8] in such markets where the world game is characterized by threat and dominance and furthermore desirable from the point of view of world welfare to the extent that they open the EC market to new competitors. There is hence clearly scope for governments' intervention in the field of industrial policy.

What Could and Should the EEC Do?

Aware of the weaknesses of the European industry, the Commission has employed all instruments and constraints of the Treaty, to favour the adjustment of industrial structures. The constraints result from the absence of specific[9] instruments for the implementation of a European industrial policy. Despite the various attempts made in the seventies to engage in more positive actions, member states have not until now endowed it with new powers or financial resources. Given that the Commission is not able to step in and rationalize declining industries or to promote sunrise activities, interventions emanate from member states. Nine-tenths of all industrial policy in the EEC take place at the national or at the regional level.

This does not mean however that the European authorities are completely powerless. They have the authority to favour harmonization of member state laws and can use the available instruments, mainly competition and commercial policy, to achieve industrial policy objectives. As article 3 of the Treaty specifies, competition is not a goal per se but a means to achieve the general socio-economic goals stated in article 2. Its maintenance is therefore justified as long as these objectives are better reached through a competitive process than by other forms of control. The Commission can exert three forms of leverage: it has the power to regulate state aids, to encourage desirable forms of cooperation between firms and is in a position to control or influence imports from third countries.

Hence whilst agreements between firms or concerted practices (art. 85), abuses of dominant positions (art. 86) and public aids to companies (art. 92) which may affect trade between member states are prohibited, art. 85(3) states that agreements or concerted practices can be exempted under the following conditions: if they contribute towards the improvement of the production or distribution of goods or promote technical and economic progress; if they allow consumers a fair share of the resulting benefits; if the restriction is necessary for the attainment of the objective and if the firms concerned are not enabled to eliminate competition with respect to a substantial part of the product in question. Alongside, art. 92(3) specifies the categories of state aids which may be regarded as being compatible with the Treaty. The Commission is thus clearly able to pursue a competition policy with industrial policy objectives.

Concerning the commercial policy, the establishment of a common external tariff implies that Member States cease to be free to determine unilaterally the level of tariffs and quota protection vis-à-vis third countries and that the level of tariffs constitutes one of the key variables in the Community's commercial stance towards the rest of the world. As stated explicitly by the Court:

> although it may be thought that at the time when the Treaty was drafted liberalization of trade was the dominant idea, the Treaty nevertheless does not form a barrier to the possibility of the Community developing a commercial policy aiming at a regulation of world markets for certain products, rather than a mere liberalization of trade.[10]

After several years of adopting a rather cautious approach, official and explicit recognition of this redirection is to be found in the last Report on Competition Policy, published in April 1985.

> In the period from 81 to 84, the Commission's aim was to bring the weight of competition policy behind the other policies designed to promote structural adjustment in the Community.

Actual implementation of European industrial policy is characterized by a shifting balance between cooperation, coordination and competiton as the main regulator of economic activity.[11] At a general level, the action of the European authorities concerns primarily industries characterized by market failures linked with externalities or increasing returns to scale. This applies to the opening-up of public procurement markets (e.g. in the field of telecommunications), to the provision of information of value for the Community as a whole - by stimulating exchanges of information or experience, by setting up multinational groups comprising R&D teams from several Member States or by working on the establishment of integrated information systems (Euro-net-Diana,[12] Insis[13]) - and to the promotion of European norms, European patents and trade-marks which aim at easing the access of firms to the whole European market. Cooperation on a transnational basis is favoured in order to avoid the development of big national champions sustained and protected by national authorities.[14] Coordination at the European level is promoted when EC has a comparative advantage in reaching international agreements to prevent escalation at a national level, e.g. in the case of subsidies or regulations in the field of technical standards and health or safety norms. As stated in the last General Report on the Activities of the Communities:

> The present main concern of European authorities remains to safeguard the dynamism of an enlarged unified market against private or public restrictive practices.

Along this line, the Green Paper on the achievement of the internal market[15] establishes a precise timetable of measures to be adopted by the Council if the objective of an unified market is to be attained in 1990.

An examination of the measures adopted in declining and progressive industries shows how the Commission stabilizes all available instruments in order to achieve consistency in the policy adopted. In declining industries, the action of the Community rests upon the need to promote an industrial structure which can face up to worldwide competition. However, in the presence of exit barriers - be they erected by firms or by governments by means of subsidies -, achievement of an orderly reduction of capacities cannot be left to market forces. Hence during the restructuring phase, state aids and cooperation between firms in the context of crisis cartels are tolerated as long as they aim at reducing structural overcapacities or at improving capacity utilization.[16] Temporary protection, by means of quotas or voluntary export restraints, is allowed in order to achieve stabilization of the import market.[17] In pace-making industries, the action of the Commission is guided by the need to promote the development and diffusion of new technologies. At the internal level, this is done by an attempt to coordinate national research efforts at the European level and by the sponsoring - in the limits of financial resources[18] - of transnational projects in specific areas. ESPRIT, a five year programme in the field of microelectronics, software technology, advanced information processing, office automation and computer-integrated manufacturing, is one of such projects. Proposals have also been made in the field of biotechnology and tele-communications services (RACE) but have not yet been approved by the

Council. In the anti-trust area, a more flexible approach is adopted with regard to constructive forms of cooperation between European firms which helps these firms to overcome barriers to entry in the field of new technologies. Hence agreements which favour the dissemination of new technology (block exemption for patent and know-how licensing) and agreements which allow the reduction in the cost of R&D, increase the size of risk which can be afforded and save time in technological cooperation (block exemption which covers agreements providing for joint R&D and joint exploitation of the results) are exempted. At the external level, duties on products, mainly chemicals, medical supplies and products of the electronics or aircraft industries have been temporarily suspended in order to ease the introduction of foreign technology.

How Far is this Policy Successful?

Whilst some success, in terms of the organization in the reduction of overcapacity and of the modernization of production facilities, seems on the way to being achieved in sectors such as steel and textiles, the Commission has difficulties in resisting the pressures on the Common Market from becoming fragmented into industries where national aids and national limits on imports from outside the Community remain substantial (e.g. the automobile sector). In pace-making industries, the action of the Communities is slowed down by the sluggishness Member States have shown in harmonizing their national regulations and their reluctance to increase the financial means of the Commission. Hence, it is only on 12 November 1984 that the Council adopted two recommendations - based on proposals made by the Commission in 1980 - on the harmonization of standards in the field of telecommunications and on the first phase of the opening-up of public telecommunication procurement contracts. In order to avoid delay in the field of harmonization of technical standards, the Commission now favours the mutual recognition of type-approval procedures against the adoption of uniform standards which was systematically blocked by recourse to the rule of unanimity. Concerning the financial means, let us observe that, although the need to increase the proportion of Community resources devoted to finance priority Community research and development activities has been several times asserted during the year 1984, it was only on 19 December 1984 that the Council did approve the proposals of the Commission and agree upon the appropriations necessary for the implementation of the different programmes. These appropriations amounted to $\frac{1}{3}$ of the amount originally estimated by the Commission. In the case of the ESPRIT programme, for example, one might question the probability of success of such a project when observing that the total funding over the five years does not even approach IBM's R&D budget for 1984 alone. Furthermore, the development of the EUREKA project, with the aim to favour high technological cooperation within Western Europe, which is under the direct control of national governments is once more a clear example of simultaneous tensions between national and European authorities and convergence of interests. As in the case of ESPRIT, a EUREKA project has to be transnational, to use advanced technology, and to offer adequate financial commitment by the companies involved. However, at the Hanover summit of November 1985, European governments were not able to take any specific decision on the site of the EUREKA secretariat, its link with the Commisssion and its future powers.[19] Bigger countries wanted to keep extra bureaucracy to a minimum, smaller countries are suspicious that without adequate channels of information, they and their industries will be by-passed. Finally, one might ask if in some cases the concern of European authorities for industrial policy objectives did not come too late. Hence in the field of video recorders, it is a little surprising to read in the last Report on Competition Policy, p. 204, that:

> The ability to respond to specific demands in new markets is crucial for the ability to survive in the consumer electronics industry. Philips and the successful Japanese firms have maintained and developed these skills by attempting to set de facto standards for new products...Philips failed to do this for their VCR system partly because other European manufacturers elected to support Japanese standards .... In contrast to the European industry, the Japanese industry succeeded in applying the strategy of an early anticipation of potential markets and a quick occupation of these markets through the creation of sufficient production capacities.

when one knows that a negative decision was taken in 1977 by the Commission concerning the exemption of an agreement between Philips and the main German producers in the field of video-recorders on the use by the Germans of common technical norms based on Philips' patents.[20]

Changes in the environment impinge on the social welfare function of the governments and on the relative concern they show for industrial policy. New external constraints have revealed the importance of dynamic efficiency as compared with static efficiency. Markets do not always favour the mobility of resources when natural or strategic barriers prevent entry or exit. Policy interventions which abolish these barriers or help economic agents to overcome them is then necessary. Increasing economic integration inside the European Community makes intervention at the EEC level more rational. However, without further progress in the field of political integration, there is a danger that Europe will remain essentially a free-trade area and never move towards an economic union. Europe will then be prevented from playing an active role in an international game the rules of which become more and more complex.

Notes

1. See the Memorandum of the Commission to the Council entitled: "Principles and General Datelines for an Industrial Policy for the Community", Brussels, 1970.
2. With the exception of petroleum, the largest European firms are now of comparable size with the largest in America, though both are significantly larger than those in Japan. (Geroski and Jacquemin, 1985a).
3. Recent developments in the economics of imperfectly competitive markets show that for a *single* country the capture of any monopoly rents on behalf of its own residents can make it desirable to pursue policies that favour its own firms and harm foreign ones (Brander and Spencer, 1984, Eaton and Grossman, 1983, Dixit, 1984).
4. The share of intra-community trade is around 50% of total trade.
5. This is a typical situation known as the prisoner's dilemma. See Johnson, 1954.
6. Dixit and Kyle (1985) have shown that, when entry is irreversible because sunk costs are important, the timing of policy actions and the degree of commitment to them become crucial. There is no scope for policy choices when firm's entry decision occurs first and the government's policies later; which will occur if the governments are in fact unable to make credible policy commitments.
7. Other examples of such strategic behaviour in the computer industry refer to Japan's entry into the market for 16K and 64K microchips, the United States' attempting entry into the markets for the 256K and megabit generations and Europe trying with the European Strategic Planning for Research and development in Information Technology (ESPRIT) to develop an alternative to these projects under way in Japan and the United States.
8. And preferable to protection as they are more difficult for commercial partners to deter.
9. In fact, two instruments are provided by the Treaty: the Regional Fund and the European Investment Bank. However, these financial means are rather limited.
10. Quoted in Steenbergen et al. (1983), p.91.
11. This is clearly stated in the last Report on Competition Policy: "Competition policy must strike a balance between reliance on market forces to maintain competition and selective intervention where necessary."
12. Direct Information Access Network for Europe.
13. Interinstitutional Network of Integrated Services.
14. As noted repeatedly in the successive Reports on Competition Policy, financial operations in the EEC remain largely confined to one country or involve a non-EEC partner when they have a transnational character.
15. European summit of Milan, 28-29 June 1985.

112

16. This has been the case in 1984 in the synthetic fibres industry and in the petrochemical sector. See the 14th Report on Competition Policy, p. 70-72.
17. Such measures have been taken in 1984 in the steel industry, the shipbuilding industry, the textile industry and the automobile industry.
18. E.C. spending on R&D amounts to 1% of total European spending (i.e. government and industrial).
19. Not mentioning the financial commitment of each member state which still remains rather vague.
20. See the 7th Report on Competition, p.110.

References

Brander J. and B. Spencer, Tariff Protection and Imperfect Competition, in Henryk Kierzkowski, ed., *Monopolistic Competition in International Trade*, Oxford: Oxford University Press, 1984.

Commission of the European Communities, *Principles and General Datelines for an Industrial Policy for the Community*. Memorandum of the Commission to the Council. Brussels, 1970.

Commission of the European Communities, *Eighteenth General Report on the Activities of the European Communities*. Brussels, February 1985.

Commission of the European Communities, *Fourteenth Report on Competition Policy*. Brussels, April 1985.

Dixit, A., International Trade Policy for Oligopolistic Industries. *Economic Journal*, March 1984, suppl., 94, 1-16.

Dixit, A. and A. Kyle, The Use of Protection and Subsidies for Entry Promotion and Deterrence. *American Economic Review*, March 1985, 75, 139-152.

Eaton, J. and G. Grossman, *Optimal Trade and Industrial Policy under Oligopoly*. Discussion Paper No. 59, Woodrow Wilson School, Princeton University, 1983.

Geroski, P.A. and A. Jacquemin, Corporate Competitiveness in Europe. *Economic Policy*, November 1985.

Geroski, P.A. and A. Jacquemin, Dominant Firms and their Alledged Decline. *International Journal on Industrial Organization*, 1985, n⁰ 2.

Hartley, K., *The Implications of National and Community Commercial Policies for the Development of the EC's Technological Industries*. CEPS Working Document n⁰ 7, 1984.

Johnson, H., Optimum Tariffs and Retaliation. *Review of Economic Studies*, February 1954, 21, 142-153.

Steenbergen J., G. De Clercq and R. Foque, *Change and Adjustment: External Relations and Industrial Policy in the European Community*. Deventer: Kluwer Law and Taxation Publishers, 1983.

PART 4
AGRICULTURAL POLICY

The Political Realities of European Agricultural Protection

PIET VAN DEN NOORT

Why Agricultural Protection in the EEC?

All capitalist countries have agricultural protection in one form or another and for various reasons. One of the best reasons is the free market's inability to reach stability and to achieve income parity for farmers because of its inherent aspects of supply and demand for agricultural products. There are also other reasons. Switzerland and Sweden have protected their agriculture so that in times of war, in which they prefer to be neutral, their agriculture can be independent. Also, the conservation of agricultural topsoil and landscape can be a reason for agricultural protection; for example as in Norway or Austria. There are countries with a long tradition of agricultural protection, such as France and Germany, but most other countries have only had such policies since the great depression of the 1930s.

Now, we could say that just as each individual country has protection for its agriculture, so the EEC has such a policy for itself. This seems to be a logical explanation, but it does not explain all problems. Why is there no common policy in other fields where each country traditionally had its own far-reaching policy measures? Why is agriculture a lone forerunner in the field of common policies? Given the ideal of unity underlying the EEC we might have expected common social, fiscal and monetary policies and also common policies in the fields of research, energy, environment or transport.

So there must be an additional factor. It is useful to remember that economic integration was a third attempt to reach political integration in Europe; that is, to agree on a policy for achieving a stable, democratic order in Europe, with reconciliation between France and Germany, no wars or revolutions, but peace and security. The earlier attempts at unification were the Marshall Plan, and the European Coal and Steel Community. The third attempt should have been the European Defence Community but this treaty was not ratified by the French National Assembly in 1954.

Integrating the economies in Europe, however, was also a means for achieving more stability and peace. Germany was all in favour of this policy, not least because it has much to gain from a large industrial market. Unlike Germany, France believed that its comparative economic strength was in agricultural production. Post-war France could therefore only agree to join the integration policies provided it could expand its markets for agricultural products in Europe, in exchange as it were, for German industrial expansion. The participation of France was essential: its government was prepared to play it hard, (it has already refused to ratify the E.D.C. Treaty) so the other countries involved thought it wise to humour France. This "grain deal" would give France access to the European agricultural markets, Germany could expand its industrial markets, and political integration could proceed.[1] The deal had, of course, its "conditions". The U.S. as a traditional grain supplier agreed to retreat a little for the greater good of political integration, but was unwilling to relinquish a considerable part of the European market. The consumers and taxpayers implicitly agreed to use more French grain provided the policy did not become too expensive i.e. prices did not become too high. Farmers in Germany, on the other hand, were willing to co-operate, providing their losses were made good. It is therefore not surprising to find these provisoes in the Treaty of Rome; in principle the deal was simple, but its implemention was only achieved by much hard work on the part of the politicians.

It is clear that France wanted to expand its agricultural production throughout the Euro-market and therefore demanded a *market policy* for agriculture and not an income-deficiency payment or social measures for farmers. To have a market means nothing without price guarantees, so the second aim of the common policy proposed for the EEC was a *price policy*. The aim was for the price of French wheat to at least meet the level of production costs in France, as otherwise a Common Market would not be an interesting proposition for the French. The EEC Member States were to give preference to French wheat: this was done by creating an artificial price difference with the world market by means of imposing a levy on imported grain ("Community preference").

It was difficult to arrive at a common acceptable price level and therefore at a common tariff or levy on grain. The French national price level was not acceptable to the Germans and the German level was not acceptable to the other Member States or to traditional overseas suppliers. So the conclusion was that the common price level should be somewhere in between and should be found during a transitional period of some twelve years!

Within the EEC, France directed its political attention to securing a watertight guarantee of the grain deal by attempting to secure detailed regulations for agricultural markets. Outside the EEC trade policy was paramount for France: for example during the Kennedy Round, when the EEC (and also the individual Member States) negotiated about tariffs, mainly on industrial goods. France, however, was not prepared to accept an attractive deal in this area unless there was also an agreement about the tariffs on agricultural products (and in fact also about the common price in the EEC). The stand taken by France was extremely effective and the EEC countries also agreed on the common price of wheat (106 "Units of Account" per ton). This, combined with the detailed market regulations, gave an almost complete common agricultural price policy (see Table 1). It was set up as a system of protection with in fact unlimited guarantees. The only flaw was that no agreement had been reached over the wheat price in years to come. Politicians played on this weak spot during prolonged negotiations (marathon sessions). No wonder France was in favour of an automatic procedure, a so-called "objective method", for fixing future prices. Although such a method was adopted, it never became a really automatic procedure!

Thus, the common agricultural price policy was necessary to obtain French co-operation, without which European integration could not proceed.

Results and Problems

The EEC has a common market policy and a common price level for many agricultural products, but if we look at the price level in national prices (applying exchange rates) we will see that the price levels and their trends differ greatly between member countries.[1] The differences are as great as before the Treaty of Rome. The price levels, however, have always been above world market price levels and were attractive for France.

Table 1. The EEC market regulation scheme

Commodities	Target price	Threshold price	Sluice gate price	Free at frontier price	Import levy	Supplementary levy	Import duty	Provision for market intervention	Provision for export refunds	Quota	Quality standards	Producers Organisation	Initial date	Date for[10] unification
Grain and grainproducts	□	□			□			□	□				1- 8-'62	1- 7-'67
Rice and riceproducts	□[1]	□		□	□			□[1]	□				1- 9-'64	1- 9-'67
Pigs and pigmeat			□		□	□		□	□				1- 8-'62	1- 7-'67
Poultry and eggs		□	□	□	□	□		□	□				1- 8-'62	1- 7-'67
Milk and dairyproducts	□[2]		□[3]	□	□			□[9]	□					29- 7-'68
Beef and veal							□	□	□	□[4]				29- 7-'68
Sugar and sugerbeets	□	□		□	□			□	□	□[5]			1- 7-'67	1- 7-'68
Oilseeds	□			□				□	□				1- 7-'67	1- 7-'67
Olive oil	□	□			□			□	□				1-11-'66	1-11-'66
Fruit and vegetables			□[6]	□		□	□		□	□[7]	□		1- 8-'62	1- 7-'68
Wine							□	□	□	□[8]	□	□	1- 8-'62	1-11-'69

1. In France and Italy; 2. Only in case of milk; 3. Guide price; 4. Levy free import quotum for frozen beef; 5. Production quotum; 6. Reference price; 7. Import quotum applicable only through a safe-guard clause procedure; 8. Import quotum; 9. Applicable for butter and skimmed milkpowder; 10. Since the dates mentioned the EEC is unified. This means that for the inner EEC-trade there are no import-levies any longer and furthermore that for the trade with third countries there are uniform import-levies and export-refunds.

France could, therefore, profit from the grain deal: it could increase its share of the European market (see Table 2). In exchange for a German industrial expansion, the French did indeed obtain a larger agricultural market, although they were faced with some competition from the Dutch, who had a high agricultural productivity and an excellent geographical position.

It is said that the CAP has only one instrument - the common price level - whereas the Treaty of Rome lays down many targets. Formally, the CAP is therefore an illogical construction; it would be logical to have a separate instrument for each target or political end. But should we look at the CAP in this way? The real and main target of the CAP was to obtain French co-operation in European policy. Market and price policies have realized this goal, though with some clashes of interest. The so-called goals of the CAP, for example as formulated in article 39 of the Treaty, can better be seen as limiting conditions, indicating *other interests* to be considered in realizing the agricultural policy.

Consumers, for example, were apprehensive of too high price levels for agricultural products. Is it true that the CAP has consumer's interests at heart and that prices are not too high? The facts are that prices at farm gate have risen less than retail food prices or retail prices for all consumer goods. Of course there has been an increase in farm prices, but it is less than other increases.[3] Without the CAP the purchasing power

Table 2. The expansion of the French agricultural market share

	1960	1967	1980	
Grains	23	32	48	mln tons
	(33)	(36)	(40)	%
Sugar	19	12	26	mln tons
	(33)	(20)	(32)	%
Milk	23	27	32	mln tons
	(26)	(28)	(28)	%

% = relative share of Euromarket

Table 3. Recent estimates of EC transfers and costs as a result of agricultural support in relation to gross domestic product and on a per person basis[1]

Period	Cost to consumers	Cost to taxpayers	Total cost to consumers and taxpayers	Cost to the economy (deadweight losses)
	As a percentage of gross domestic product			
	%	%	%	%
EC-9				
1974-trough	0.6	1.1	1.7	0.16
1978-peak	1.8	1.0	2.8	0.48
EC-10				
1983	1.2	1.0	2.2	0.32
Average				
1973-83	1.3	1.0	2.3	0.30
	Per person (in 1982 values)			
	ECU	ECU	ECU	ECU
EC-9				
1974-trough	48	84	132	12
1978-peak	163	85	248	43
EC-10				
1983	112	90	202	29
Average				
1973-83	112	86	198	27

[1] After allowance for the estimated effect of EC support policies on world market prices for major agricultural products.

Source: see note 8.

Fig. 1. (Abstract from Table 6) EC own resources: limits and expenditure commitments

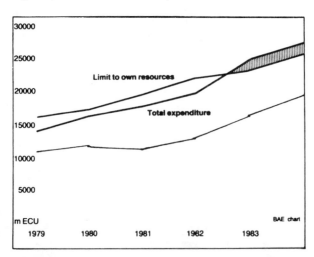

Table 4. Guarantee expenditure by economic category

Year	Storage[a]	Aids[b]	Other[c]	Co-responsibility receipts from milk	Export refunds[d]	Total guarantee expenditure[e]
	m ECU	m ECU	m ECU	m ECU	m ECU	m ECU
1979	1658	3779	116	—94	4982	10441
	(15.9)	(36.2)	(1.1)	(—0.9)	(47.7)	(100.0)
1980	1617	3928	298	—223	5695	11315
	(14.3)	(34.7)	(2.6)	(—2.0)	(50.4)	(100.0)
1981	1631	4343	436	—478	5209	11141
	(14.6)	(39.0)	(3.9)	(—4.3)	(46.8)	(100.0)
1982	1818	5468	603	—537	5054	12406
	(14.6)	(44.1)	(4.9)	(—4.3)	(40.7)	(100.0)
1983	2893	7281	712	—527	5560	15920
	(18.2)	(45.7)	(4.5)	(—3.3)	(34.9)	(100.0)
1984 (supplementary budget)	3583	7942	1130	—972	6718	18401
	(19.5)	(43.2)	(6.1)	(—5.3)	(36.5)	(100.0)

[a] Includes rebates on storage of, for example, butter for pastry-making and skimmed milk used in animal feed - in accordance with the budget nomenclature. [b] Aids to producers, processing aids, marketing aids for products, MCAs for intra-EC trade and guidance premiums (195m ECU in 1983). [c] Distillation and withdrawals. [d] Includes MCAs for extra-EC trade. [e] Including the common organisation of the market in fisheries. There may be minor differences in total expenditure in various tables due to the different treatment regarding payment of previous years' accounts.

Note: Figures in parentheses are proportions of total guarantee expenditure.

Source: Commission of the European Communities (1983a, 1984c, 1985a).

Table 5. Community revenue and expenditure

Item	1974 m EUA	1975 m EUA	1976 m EUA	1977 m EUA	1978 m EUA	1979 m ECU	1980 m ECU	1981 m ECU	1982[a] m ECU	1983[b] m ECU	1984[c] m ECU
						Revenue					
Customs duties	2737	3151	4064	3927	4391	5189	5906	6392	6815	6989	7884
Agricultural levies[d]	330	590	1164	1778	2279	2143	2002	1747	2228	2295	3172
Value-added tax						4738	7259	9188	12000	13699	14377
Other	1969	2473	2765	2779	5507	2532	899	1122	197	1783	1816
Total	5036	6214	7993	8484	12177	14602	16066	18449	21241	24766	27249
(Change[e])	(5)	(23)	(29)	(6)	(44)	(20)	(10)	(15)	(15)	(17)	(10)
VAT percentage						0.79	0.73	0.79	0.92	1.00	1.00
						Expenditure					
Agriculture											
– Guarantee Section[f]	3278	4821	5365	6167	9279	10434	11306	10988	12406	15898	18333
– Guidance Section	128	184	218	297	324	403	601	576	548	688	675
Social Fund	238	136	256	317	285	596	735	746	1019	1431	1644
Regional Fund	—	91	277	373	255	513	727	799	2988	2431	1455
Co-operation with developing countries	169	324	137	216	265	405	508	858	791	981	897
Research and energy investment	78	116	118	143	192	254	290	359	454	1441	1740
Reimbursement to member states	284	354	422	665	662	900	1222	2394	1068	1120	1155
Other sectors	5	9	24	31	36	88	78	128	35	106	
Administration	337	375	420	497	677	773	820	944	701	760	811
Total	4516	6411	7238	8705	11973	14367	16290	17792	20012	24871	27249
(Agriculture's share[g])	(75)	(78)	(77)	(74)	(80)	(75)	(73)	(65)	(65)	(67)	(70)

[a] Out-turn. [b] After supplementry budget no. 2 for expenditure. [c] Amending and supplementary budget, 1984. [d] Includes sugar levies. [e] Figures in parentheses are percentage changes from previous year. [f] There may be minor differences in total expenditure in various tables due to the different treatment regarding payment of previous years' accounts. [g] Figures in parentheses are proportions of agricultural expenditure in total expenditure.

Sources: Commission of the European Communities (peronal communication, December 1983; 1985a); Office for Official Publication of the European Communities (1984b).

of the consumers would have been higher. They have been paying about 2.5 percent of national income as income transfer to farmers, but without CAP there would have been a similar (national) transfer to income, so we should only look at the additional aspects. The consumers also had some interest in supply and in self-sufficiency. The achievement of self-sufficiency is remarkable. For almost all products the degree of self-sufficiency has increased considerably since the inception of the EEC, often to figures exceeding 100 percent. As a consequence, ample supplies have been available for consumers, but in their role as taxpayers, consumers have also paid out large sums. This has taken place in a period in which all countries have been experiencing serious problems with government finances. So when expenditures of the EC reached the limits of the own resources, we had a problem and also a political possibility to change the CAP, see Fig 1. Foreign consumers have benefited from this, because food has become cheap and this has improved welfare in some countries although foreign exporters have suffered: they complain of dumping. For developing countries the repercussions are mixed: industrialization policies benefit, but those countries that give priority to agricultural development have suffered.

Some *politicians and economists* were afraid of the high real costs of protection: too many resources in agriculture, a bad structure and low productivity. According to article 39, this should be prevented and in this the agricultural policies have been successful. Since the Treaty of Rome was signed, there has been an enormous outflow of agricultural labour (about 4% per year), an increase in farm size and a rise in technical productivity (by between 3 to 5% per year): this rate is as good as can be found in industry.

It is true, however, that a consequence of price protection was that labour that could better have been employed in other parts of the economy was retained in agriculture - at the expense of the domestic product of the EEC. So there are real costs involved with the CAP. These are not more than 0.5 percent of domestic product, see Table 3. In the period of growth 1965-1975 this was not a large burden, particularly when it is remembered that without the CAP we would have had national price policies that would also have had their real costs. The additional real costs of the CAP are therefore around 0.2 percent of domestic product. The real benefits of free trade between Member States was according to Scitovsky[7] perhaps 0.1 to 0.5 percent of domestic product. In comparison with these benefits the costs of agricultural protection were relatively high. This could only be accepted as the political and "dynamic" benefits were considerable. It is not surprising that protests against the CAP become serious again in the 1980s when the economic growth, the dynamic benefits of integration and even the political benefits seemed to be small.

Farmers were afraid of a loss in their position. In general the relative position of farmers increased. Farmers' income grew considerably in the 1960s and 1970s but there still is a disparity of incomes.[1]

So there really have been problems: real costs, income transfers, budgetary costs, income disparity, disturbance of international trade or development policies. Nevertheless, the EEC has obtained six new members: Greece, U.K., Eire, Denmark, Spain and Portugal. The recent entrance of two new members (Spain and Portugal) will lead to additional problems in all these areas.

Solutions and Prospects

Looking back, we can say that the European policy to arrive at peace, stability and democracy in Europe has been a priority. The economic policies can be seen as a means of achieving this goal. The agricultural policy is part of this policy and is also a concrete example of a complicated and costly means of achieving that goal.

The situation is now very different from that in the 1950s. We are no longer concerned with reconstruction and reconciliation; East-West relations are also different. We are concentrating more on daily, technical problems than on dealing with high ideals. Nevertheless, we have grave social and economic problems and it is surprising that there are not more common actions against unemployment, environmental destruction, energy problems, or for scientific research and for strategies of development. The entry into the EEC of Spain and Portugal also raised important aspects in the idealistic desire to strengthen democracy in Europe. But again, even these important policies are overshadowed by a large number of more or less technical problems concerning vegetables, grain, wine, money and all kinds of foreign relations in the Mediterranean.

I believe that France and the northern areas of the EEC are now in a similar position as Germany was in 1957. Spain and Portugal have special agricultural interests, just as the founder EEC members now have industrial interests. It is interesting indeed to "swap markets". It is even questionable whether France did in fact have such a large economic interest in grain exports as was said at the time[2]; but nowadays even France is an industrial nation and should give Spain a chance, in exchange for participation in a large industrial market. The CAP has the historical rôle of improving and accelerating economic and political integration and should not become a brake on these policies.

Many proposals for new policies have been put forward and some have indeed been incorporated in the CAP. I believe it is unwise to continue changing policies each season. There are still many alternatives open to the CAP. Let us consider some major examples.

One of the oldest alternatives is a *structural policy* instead of an extensive price policy. Price levels could be lower if we had a modern well-structured agriculture. Thus in the late 1960s Commissioner Mansholt proposed a plan to achieve this in agriculture. The idea was to accelerate the migration of labour out of and modernization of agriculture. This Plan ran into much opposition because of its flaws. For example, it had a low rate of return, needed a large budget, did not consider the unfavourable social consequences of migration and it disregarded the vested interests of the agricultural lobby. To-day we could also use a better organized agriculture, but a new Mansholt Plan would be no wise policy because an additional outflow of labour from agriculture would be unprofitable and the modernisation of agriculture would also lead to more production and more surpluses, which is also unprofitable. Additional structural measures are therefore not the solution.

An effective measure is to *decrease price levels* or levels of protection. The high price levels are the real cause of surpluses and their consequences. Many would gain from lower prices, but farming and some agribusiness would not. The income position of farmers is an important aspect of agricultural policies in Europe and this policy line is therefore not generally acceptable in real politics e.g. when applied to cereals in 1985 it created much political tension in the Community. Comparable proposals that have been considered have involved *increases in import prices*, especially of feedstuffs.

To have the advantages of low prices but also to maintain income protection and the social position of farmers, Professor van Riemsdijk proposed a *direct income payment system* in which the loss of income resulting from the lower prices would be compensated for by direct income payments to farmers. These payments would only be made for a limited period of time, at most twenty years, and only to farmers up to 65 years of age. This would give a stimulus to improve farming, because after that transitional period low prices would rule the agricultural economy and to survive, farmers would need large and modern farms. This plan was also debated but rejected, because it also had a low rate of return, needed a large budget and would have led to a large migration, with all its social and political repercussions. Today, all these problems would still follow such a policy to an even greater degree, because any additional outmigration is not at all profitable. Any increase in the budget for agriculture would meet great political opposition.

Another method is to restrict production by imposing production quotas per country and per farmer. There is a large range of possibilities in this field. The super levy system now in use in the dairy sector is perhaps the best known example. It is a purely technical measure. It restricts production and therefore decreases the budget costs of the CAP but without the basic systematic improvements that the above mentioned alternative policies promised to give. The restrictive measures that in fact have been taken for sugar, milk and to grains or cereals have changed the CAP system from an unlimited guarantee to a limited one. This is already a considerable change when we realize how strongly the farmers are organized compared with all other interest groups.

Interesting proposals are also *to take marginal land out of agricultural production* and use it for timber production or for recreation. The difficulty with this policy idea is to find in fact this marginal land. In the Netherlands e.g. you cannot find any considerable area of this type of land and it is said that timber production is not profitable and therefore not an attractive alternative to milk production. But in several other regions it could indeed be a splendid idea, to increase alternative production. The problem with labour extensive products like timber is that you have to find new means to protect employment now found in the CAP. This would require an additional social policy. It is interesting to note that such policies of new uses of agricultural land could have a positive effect on the environment.

Each of these measures has its variations. So in theory, there are many alternative proposals for solving the CAP problems. Among economists there is a strong tendency to try to find the optimal instrument in that series of solutions by estimating the total net effect on welfare of the Community each instrument has, and selecting the highest-scoring measure. The difficulty with this procedure, based on Professor Tinbergen's theory of economic policy,[5] is, that there is in fact no social welfare function or no such function can be specified and estimated. So it is no use looking for an instrument or measure that will lead to the maximum value of this function.[4] This method can only be applied to individual or partial preferences but will not indicate the social preferences of a nation or the Community as a whole. The real selection can therefore only be done by other, that is *political means*. This conclusion is too often overlooked by economists. It is a pity political science has no empirically tested theory on political decision-making on this level. What we can say is that the political selection process in Europe is dominated by the "unanimity rule" in the Council of Ministers (this is a result of President de Gaulle's policy towards the EEC in 1965). This Council is a kind of coalition government of the EEC: ten ministers working towards common decisions. The bartering of votes between them is an obvious way of reaching agreements. To reach unanimity will require more strength and more exchange or trade-offs than simple majority rule would require. Because in practice this Council only deals with agricultural affairs and not all manner of other affairs (as a national cabinet must do) the political bargaining will lead to ever more measures in the agricultural field, each time making agricultural policy more expensive. So if we could find more common policies (e.g. for energy, environment, unemployment, research) and if we could really apply majority rules we could get easier and cheaper political solutions for agriculture too.

An enlarged EEC cannot continue with its agricultural policies in the same way as it did before the entry of Spain and Portugal. Continuing to increase price levels is leading us into grave problems. We must realize also that small farmers, with only small means of production (of which there are many especially in Southern Europe) can never be given a reasonable income by price policies only. High prices lead also to large income differences within agriculture and have a tendency to lead to high rents and land prices. We will need a freeze on prices and production for some time. To prevent social problems we could try to secure a reasonable income for farmers by introducing i.e. income deficiency payments. This *social measure* could even be part of the national social policy and therefore be completely financed out of the national budget. If this is done we will have reached the watershed between the economic and the social aspects of agricultural policies. In future, this social aspect could better be dealt with separately. This idea has become part of the new proposals of Commissioner Andriessen to reform the Common Agricultural Policy as formulated in his Greenbook. These proposals are now at the start of the political decision making process. Experience with former reform proposals show that it will be not simple and easy.[6] But this time it must have positive results, otherwise the Common Agricultural Policy will become the breaking point in European policies.

References

1. Coffey, P. (ed.), *Main Economic Policy Areas of the EEC*, Martinus Nijhoff Publishers, the Hague, 1983, pp. 1-26.
2. Harvey, D.R., National Interests and the CAP, *Food Policy*, August 1982.
3. Meester, G., Doeleinden, instrumenten en effecten van het landbouwbeleid in de EG, Landbouw-Economisch Instituut, Den Haag, 1980.
4. Van den Noort, P.C., The problem of optimum policy choice in European agriculture, *Neth. J. of Agr. Sci.* 31 (1983), pp. 93-97.
5. Tinbergen, J., *On the theory of economic policy*, North-Holland, Amsterdam, 1952.
6. Pelkmans, J. (ed.), *Can the CAP be reformed?*, IEAP, Maastricht, 1985.
7. Scitovsky, Tibor, *Economic Theory and Western European Integration*, Unwin, London, 1958, p. 67.
8. Agricultural Policies in the European Community. Their Origions, Nature and Effects on Production and Trade. Policy Monograph No.2. Bureau of Agricultural Economics, Canberra, 1985.

Some Structural Aspects of Mexican Agriculture and the Possibility of Reaching a Complementary Arrangement in Food Trade with Europe

ALFONSO CEBREROS

1. Changes in Demography and Food Production

For almost four decades from 1930 to 1966 Mexico's agricultural production was able to support its food consumption needs and was a dynamic factor in the country's growth in employment and in the generation of foreign exchange. From 1930 to 1946 farming production grew at a rate of 3.5 percent per annum as opposed to a population which grew at 2.2 percent. During the twenty years that followed, the population began to increase to an annual rate of 3.2 percent, but the agricultural sector, however, showed an even more dynamic growth which reached an average annual rate of 7 percent.

This meant a considerable improvement in the per capita availability of foodstuffs and in the sector's contribution to economic development in general. The primary sector in particular laid the foundations for urban and industrial development, making real and monetary financing possible and creating a broad domestic market as well.

From 1966 to 1980 this ratio was inverted drastically. To start with, population growth was sustained or increased even more while growth in agricultural production began to decline, reaching an annual rate of 2 percent. Thus, two of the country's two major problems in this area were aggravated, viz, malnutrition among broad sectors of the population and a dependence on food from abroad.

An analysis of events occurring during this period shows that Mexico prematurely abandoned the priority it had previously given to farming development and that economic crises do not arise from one moment to the next but are derived from structural factors that have evolved over a more prolonged period of time. As the farming sector began to lose impetus, the decline in the number of jobs available and in rural income speeded up urbanization and deformed it in the process, with a very high social and economic cost.

A paradoxical situation was also created whereby the producers of basic foodstuffs were the very ones who suffered from the worst malnutrition. One could say that many of Mexico's economic achievements of the last few decades have been at the expense of decapitalization and dehumanization of the farming industry. Although, lately, Mexico has managed to gradually reduce its population growth, it is nonetheless an unavoidable fact that its labour force will double and its urban population will triple. The country's capacity to create jobs and produce food will constantly be under strain.

It is Mexico's growing urbanization that is perhaps its most important change qualitatively. Despite this, however, the rural population doubled in absolute terms between 1940 and 1980. During the last decade its growth rate fell to 1 percent. Nevertheless, the important thing is that the number of inhabitants in rural areas still continues to increase. For this reason better job opportunities should be made available in Mexico's farming communities.

With the reactivation of food production, there will also be the possibility of creating productive employment in rural areas. This is even more true where an integrated approach to rural development is adopted. However, it is important to remember that there will be growing pressure on urban jobs and that in the long term the only answer is very efficient industrialization and the creation of a reasonably productive services sector. For the moment, the limitations imposed on the country by the present crisis as regards investment in high cost projects with long lead times points to the advisability of taking advantage of the short and medium-term opportunities available for rural development.

The proliferation of settlements living below subsistence level cannot be allowed to continue in rural areas. In order to satisfy the growing demand for food, farming production must necessarily be modernized along with a major transference of rural population to urban settlements.

The fact that the rural population continues to lose relative importance does not mean that the farmers' economy should remain as weak as it is. On the contrary, for Mexico to be able to carry out this demographic and economic transition efficiently and equitatively, farming must be capable of providing a thrust to the economy, it must be a profitable business, a dignified means of earning a living and effectively provide the food needed for the country's development.

With the 5 percent growth of the urban population per annum over the last four years, there has been both a quantitative and a qualitative change in the demand for foodstuffs. Urbanization brings about an increase in family income and with this the creation of a rising middle class whose consumer habits and expectations are strongly influenced by other social classes and countries. At the same time, the city offers the best of the food production and much greater diversification to the consumer. Generally speaking, points out Nicolás Reig of the National Autonomous University of Mexico, the "urbanization effect" is particularly noticeable in the substitution of maize for wheat and in an increase in the consumption of animal products.

This gives rise to an unwanted competition between the production of food for direct human consumption and that produced for animal feed in a step prior to this. The competition between sorghum and maize and between extensive cattle farming and agriculture are examples of this.

The problems that have arisen in this area can only be solved through an approach involving ample thrust to be given to the rapid increase of farming frontiers and production along with the integration and intensification of farming activities. Cattle raising and agriculture can no longer continue to be rival activities. They must evolve towards a situation where they are complementary and help raise the land's productivity, for future expansion will necessarily be constrained by the high cost involved in opening up new areas.

During the last few decades there has been an irreversable change in the Mexican diet. The production or consumption of certain basic foods should not be discouraged in favour of others. An effort must be made to attend to all the legitimate needs and expectations of the consumer in all income brackets.

On the other hand, it is important also to try and avoid certain bad eating habits that tend to come hand in hand with urbanization such as the consumption of more costly industrialized products with either very little or no nutritional value.

In short, overcoming the malnutrition that is common in rural areas or marginal urban zones as well as attending to the growing demands of the urban population implies a very great effort in promoting farming growth and productivity. Not only is political will in the form of government programmes needed, but also of utmost importance is the general consensus of the whole population, particularly the urban, that it is a top priority national project involving shared costs and sacrifices, particularly on the part of those who can afford to pay the real price of this adjustment.

2. Structural Changes in Mexico's Agriculture

The relative deterioration in Mexico's farming production both from the point of view of population growth as well as gross national product responds to a combination of factors, the most significant of which will be commented upon below. These factors involve considering the farming sector as part of the model and the strategy for economic growth, with special attention to certain policies together with a certain degree of success in creating an urban middle class that demands constant improvement in its level of income and of consumption.

a) Population and Surface Area Harvested

One of the major factors influencing the deterioration in Mexico's agricultural sector has been the demographic pressure placed on the land and which has increased noticeably during the last few decades. While from 1935 to 1959 the number of inhabitants per hectare fell from 3.6 to 2.9, by 1981 it had risen again to 4.7. If we examine this from the other way round, i.e. as a function of farming population, we can see that the surface area harvested per unit of rural work force increased steadily from 1935 to 1969. After 1970 the opposite tendency was observed. A comparison of the cultivated surface area per farm worker on a world wide scale shows that Mexico's coefficient is around 25 percent lower than the average for Latin America.

Independently of the need for programmes aimed at raising productivity in farming, it is clear that the amount of available farm land must be increased and at the same time special attention must be given to irrigation, for despite sustained investment in the field for prolonged periods, 75 percent of Mexico's agriculture continues to be seasonal. Owing to the sustained growth in harvested area in irrigated zones, seasonal areas are now subject to major fluctuations from one year to the next. Mexican agriculture is highly susceptible to climatic changes and as the climate is predominantly dry with rain only in very small areas, farming production shows sharp variations also.

The amount of land with access to irrigation has grown continuously but it is still insufficient for the country's needs. From 1946 to 1966 the figure went from 420 thousand hectares to around 1.8 million. By 1982 there were 2.9 million hectares of irrigated land.* This trend has slowed down lately due to the high cost of irrigation districts, particularly those that demand major hydraulic works, and the current shortage of public finances.

Thus, increasing the amount of arable land available must consider three basic lines of action: incorporating land for farming using current technological methods, broadening the cultivated area by introducing new crops into the humid tropical areas as well as the semi-arid zones, and making use of cattle lands with an integrated approach combining agrarian and production policies.

b) Public Investment in Farming Promotion

The above-mentioned situation is clearly associated with the growing importance of farming promotion within the total public investment. From 1934 to 1952, farming's average share of the budget was maintained at around 18 percent, with a slight tendency to increase. During the years from 1953 to 1958 the figure dropped to less than 14 percent and then fell over the next twelve years to between 10 and 11 percent.

During the latter period, as we will see in more detail later on, real guarantee prices on the major food products stagnated. Serious decapitalization thus occurred in the farming sector in order to subsidize the urban consumer and industrial development at the expense of rural production. Although from 1970 to 1980 around 18 percent of public investment was channelled into promoting farming, the fact that guarantee prices did not catch up, together with institutional factors, made the farming sector's recovery very slow and irregular.

All this made it necessary to reflect on the importance rural development should have within the country's economic and social strategy. Also to be considered is the fact that the extreme social inequality that exists in Mexico is due to a large extent to the situations just mentioned. The improvement in the lot of the middle classes after the sixties was accompanied by a deterioration in that of the low-income group, made up basically of peasant farmers and the marginal urban population which had moved towards the cities not because of any dynamic growth there but because of inadequate rural development. The result was

---

*This refers to the hydraulic infrastructure built directly by the State. The grand national total including the area improved by the State and that irrigated with the help of private investment comes to 5,4 million hectares.

almost always a clash between the peasant farmers' ideology and culture and the urban life style.

In short, we can see that the evolution of the food-producing sector within the Mexican economy over the last two decades and the lack of sufficient support given to it largely determine the nature of the problem today. Furthermore, owing to the fact that for a long time food production was held in check, certain conditions have been created which have led to hoarding and speculating with foodstuffs becoming a traditional means of acquiring large amounts of capital and a cause of inflation.

Under the present circumstances it will be virtually impossible for the country to undergo sure and sustained development if we do not manage to catch up with the rest of the advanced countries in food production and create an effective and prosperous rural economy. Without strong primary activities, efficient modernization is impossible. We are not unaware of the major effort that this implies. To give an example, the recovery of the farming sector's dynamic growth demands that irrigated surface area be doubled within the next 15 years. Calculations made by Manuel Aguilera point out that this would require around 50 percent of the farming sector's earnings from production and therefore would be impossible to finance without funds being transferred from the urban-industrial sector.

Mexico's global progress is in danger of being restrained if a national effort is not made to cover the debt we all owe to the rural sector, particularly to the peasant farmer who grows the basic crops for feeding the nation.

c) Productivity and Distribution of Basic Crops

If, despite the above-mentioned constraints, modest farming growth has been sustained, it is due mainly to the fact that yield has increased steadily over the last 20 years and compensated for the fall in the rate at which harvested areas have increased. Data provided by K. Shwedel show major increases in the production per hectare of maize, this being 47.8 percent for the last 15 years. Wheat has increased 53.3 percent, beans 31.9 percent, rice 27.1 percent and sorghum 24.9 percent. The comaparison is made between the period from 1965-69 and that from 1979-83. These 5 crops represent 61.4 percent of the harvested area and 43.4 percent of the value of agricultural production for 1981.

Of all the major crops, there was only a slight drop in the productivity of soya bean of 3.2 percent for the period mentioned. The sustained growth in average yield was due basically to the increased availability and distribution of improved inputs, the effect of which was far greater than technological changes, except in the case of wheat. Shwedel also explains that another major change in the Mexican farming sector over the last two decades was the increase in cattle production and in the agricultural activities related to it. The poultry and pork farming industries substantially increased their per unit scale of operations to become modern commercial businesses.

Growth in cattle production and in its supporting industries had major implications for the distribution of crops. The use of land for basic crops dropped from 73 to 64 percent from the mid-sixties up to 1983. On the other hand, fodder crops, such as sorghum, showed a sustained increase as they went from 2 percent to nearly 13 percent of the total surface area harvested during the same period. Although more attention has been paid to producing basic crops over the last decade and the demand for meat has fallen with the resulting decline in cattle production, the former sector represents almost half of Mexico's agricultural production if forrage is included.

d) Rural Saving

All the previously mentioned factors have combined to severely limit savings in the rural sector, especially with the peasant farmers. Decapitalization has led to underemployment and an increase in the number of small farmsteads. The latest information available shows that nearly 50 percent of all rural producers are peasant farmers living below subsistence level and an additional 16 percent barely reach subsistence level. By definition, this large sector cannot generate a surplus that can help capitalize the farming sector. All in all these farmers have barely 20 percent of the available capital at their disposal and although their productivity in the use of the same is high, it is still insufficient due to the fact that the first group of farmers work only an average of less than two hectares each and the second group only 6 hectares.

Mexican agricultural growth is characterized by its polarization, which is derived from the tendency to concentrate productive resources, and therefore production, in one area. This has led to clearly differentiated commercial farming and subsistence agricultural sectors. In both the group of private farm owners and the peasant farmers that work their "ejidos"* heavy population density exists. The latter system is characterized by an increase in exploitation of the individual, which, due to rural population growth, has produced a phenomenon known as "ejido breakup". This particular characteristic has converted the ejidal system into a kind of small farmstead system, despite existing legal regulations or the objectives behind its creation.

This rural production structure is, of course, the basis of the social inequality that exists in the rural areas themselves and between them and the urban settlements. Inequality can only be eliminated through a capitalization strategy favouring the least protected rural producer. To be effective it would require that progress be made in organizing and creating production units that allow the introduction of new farming and administrative techniques, the joint utilization of strategic capital goods and the gradual integration into the agro-industrial process.

e) Production and Guarantee Prices

Due to the importance of guarantee prices in determining some of the aspects just mentioned it would be worthwhile going into this a little further. K. Appendini, a researcher at El Colegio de México, pointed out the "during the period of stabilizing development a ceiling prices policy prevailed". In other words, there was a price control policy designed to hold down the price of those foodstuffs required for the country's growing industrialization and urbanization. This was a determining factor in the net transfer of capital from the farming sector to the rest of the economy and was the major cause of the prostration of farming production during the years that followed.

In 1972 real guarantee prices for crops were well below 1950 prices. Although afterwards a certain degree of priority was given to the farming sector once more in terms of public investment, the resulting recovery in production was still insufficient to satisfy existing demand. After 1974 guarantee prices were set every year, but very few products bettered their real price. The tendency then was towards a decline, only to improve again in 1981, although the former maximum levels were never reached again.

The relative prices of forrage crops were constantly maintained above those for basic products from 1966 until 1973, and then sporadically

---

*TN An ejido is a plot of land leased to the peasant farmer by the government for an indefinite period of time for farming purposes.

until 1979. In 1981 the price of oleaginous seeds was still higher than that for basic crops. Although the guarantee price policy followed for the last four years has given preferential support to basic foodstuff production it still continues to be an unprofitable business, a situation that is incompatible with the country's prime objective of recovering its self-sufficiency in food production. The changes that occurred in crop distribution have not been modified either.

The current government administration has begun to revise prices twice a year. In 1984 there was at last a real increase but it was still not enough for prices to catch up. It is necessary to continue with this policy as there are costs that the government cannot absorb completely. Furthermore, this should be complemented with top priority being granted to the rural sector in the assignment of economic resources.

3. Current Outlook for Mexico's Food-Producing Sector

Over the last twenty years, after a similar highly productive period, Mexican agriculture's growth rate dropped to an annual average of 2 percent, which was lower than the country's population growth rate. The long-term trends and the immediate effects of the economic crisis have brought about a revaluation of the importance of the food-producing sector in the government's economic and social development strategy. In October 1983 the Programa Nacional de Alimentación (National Alimentary Program - PRONAL) was introduced.

The recent response in food production to economic reorganization policies has shown this to be one of the best ways of recovering growth capacity and of providing a timely solution to the problem of modifying production and distribution structures that have proven to be anachronistic and inefficient. Although there was a heavy fall in the national product for 1983 and economic growth fell during 1984, the farming sector continued to grow, and on average surpassed average population growth rates. This modest improvement will probably continue during 1985.

Rural producers have shown their capacity to respond to the incentives provided by the State. Guarantee prices have been revised more often and efforts have been made to keep them more in line with real prices. Although not always possible in all cases, the general trend is clear - to increase economic resources assigned to the rural sector and close the gap between the rural and urban standard of living. This strategy will be further reinforced with the introduction of the Programa

Nacional de Desarrollo Rural Integral (National Program for Integrated Rural Development).

Food production strategy has concentrated on those farming products where there is a shortage, mainly maize, oleaginous seeds, sorghum and milk. Mexico has been self-sufficient over the last two years in wheat, beans, sugar, eggs and meat. Medium-term forecasts indicate that the country will either attain or manage to sustain self-sufficiency in the major grains and cereals, including maize, but not so in oil and vegetable fats which had a 354 thousand ton deficit in 1985 to be reduced to 242 thousand in 1988. Oleaginous pastes have a deficit also which will increase from 987 thousand tons to 1.105 million tons. The shortage of sorghum remains at around 2 million tons and milk production will increase slightly leaving a deficit of 1600 million litres.

On the other hand, major increases in growth rate have been forecast for those products where Mexico already has exporting capacity, i.e. fruit, 3.6 percent, garden produce 4 percent, cocoa 3.8 percent and coffee 1.1 percent. Bees' honey will, however, suffer a major decline due to the recent arrival of the African bee in Mexico. The fishing sector has managed to overcome the difficult economic conditions and natural phenomena it was subject to during 1982 and 1983. The fishing fleet and on-shore facilities have continued to operate despite problems in the use of installed capacity. Some of the projects under way were completed and other new major ones were commenced. Fishing production increased 9.8 percent in 1984, which was well above the average for national economic activity. The basic strategy here consists of giving priority to those products whose easy availability and the economies they create will allow adequate supply at reasonable prices. The PRONAL is particularly interested in traditionally massive catches, sardines, tuna fish, those produced with aquiculture as well as fresh water fish. The production of food from the sea will grow to almost a million tons by 1988, with an annual average increase of 14 percent. Furthermore, it is expected that the tuna fish catch will double.

The food manufacturing industry has also managed to achieve a positive growth rate over the last two years, despite a severe fall in the manufacturing sector's production. The rates are, however, lower than the population growth rate. The Mexican food industry is mainly in the hands of private companies, whether local or foreign. State participation is minimal and is dedicated mainly to price control over basic products, although it is involved in 100 percent of the country's sugar production, 30 percent of its maize flour, 50 percent of its tinned fish products, 10 percent of its wheat flour, 14 percent of its oil and 25 percent of its industrialized milk.

Sufficient installed capacity exists already to industrialize wheat, rice oleaginous seeds and animal feed. It is absolutely essential to continue modernizing the sugar industry in order to raise productivity. It is also necessary to speed up maize flour production through direct State participation. The installed capacity in fish as well as milk processing facilities has increased recently and there should be no problem in the short term. However, a general reactivation of the demand should be anticipated, particularly considering the strategic importance of both of these products as a source of animal protein.

4. Recent Trends in Trade between Mexico and the EEC

The evolution of economic relations between Mexico and the EEC has undergone significant changes over the last few years, but one would not say the relationship is satisfactory. Mexican exports have increased four-fold in five years, due almost exclusively to oil. On the other hand, imports which had shown rapid growth earlier in the decade fell substancially due to a combination of commercial, financial and monetary factors.

Although Mexico's trade balance is at present favourable, oil's excessive participation tends to distort the whole outlook and the possibility of improving commercial interchange and of joint-investment should not be overlooked. One of the fields that deserves more attention is precisely that of food products. Here, trade has been rather small and somewhat irregular, and a fair dose of political goodwill on both sides will be needed along with the ability to take action to take advantage of certain mechanisms that have not been used to their full potential. In addition to this, both parties must be fully aware of the major obstacles that will have to be faced in this area.

Over the last five years Mexican food exports to the EEC have increased more or less steadily. Imports have fallen considerably although initially they had tended to rise. However, these trends are not really significant as we are talking about very low figures which even at the best of times, such as in 1981, barely amounted to 180 million dollars in all.

On the other hand, there is very little diversification in this interchange. Raw coffee is by far Mexico's biggest export product and milk powder and associated butyric fats its main import. One could perhaps also mention honey as another product of some importance, whereas all the rest are either very small, irregular or sporadic.

Certain geographic, historic and economic factors combined explain this situation. On the European side there are protectionist policies which affect manufactured products, together with a particularly rigid agricultural policy. Supplies tend to come from traditional sources and producers from certain other countries are given preferential treatment, particularly African nations. On the Mexican side, production is not controlled through an export programme and there is very little quality control. A factor concerning both parties is the lack of attention paid to improving reciprocal transport systems.

The outlook for Europe's presence in Mexico's food industry is not particularly encouraging. The European Economic Community's investment in Mexico barely amounts to 20 percent of total foreign investment. Furthermore, less than 6 percent of this corresponds to foodstuffs, an area dominated mainly by the United States. Although we are aware of the problems and obstacles involved in increasing commercial and industrial interchange, this should not lead us to conclude rashly that little can be done in this respect. On the other hand, we do foresee that a sustained effort must be made, with a long-term viewpoint and mutual political concern that reflects the conviction that it is worthwhile for both parties to work together.

It is also important that these efforts be determined not only by market forces but that clearly defined work be carried out in determining specific areas and projects to be addressed, where on occasions success will depend on the support the respective government have provided. To give this support it will be necessary to establish new and better ways of cooperation and of providing technical and financial assistence that will enhance the economic and social characteristics of the projects in question. More specifically, it must be an accepted fact that in dealings with economically unequal partners, there must be a fairly good dose of cooperation on the part of the more advanced of them.

5. Areas where Complementary Trade is Possible

I. Products

a) Oleaginous seeds
Mexico's high per capita consumption of oil, the priority given to

self-sufficiency in basic grains and the fact that most of Mexico's oleaginous seed crops are complementary or competitive with others indicates that the country will continue to import significant amounts of this product. The dependence is related more to the grower aspect rather than at the level of industry, as the latter in general has sufficient installed capacity to satisfy demand on the basis of imported raw materials. However, new strategically located projects are planned in which foreign investment may be incorporated in association with Mexican producers or even the state-owned sector.

The problems involved in achieving self-sufficiency in traditional crops and the possibility of improving existing physical resources point to the need to diversify both internal and external supply sources. The most immediate possibilities lie in developing sunflower seed crops which already exist on a very small scale, along with colza and the African palm. Europe is technologically very advanced in these areas, particularly in the case of the latter two crops, from the point of view of both growing and industrialization. Mexico has already elaborated projects involving African palm crops for certain regions and the facilities that need to be installed. This is a field in which foreign investment could be combined with government technical and financial assistence programmes within a framework of economic cooperation.

Additionally, it is of interest to Mexico to incorporate the technology needed to utilize more efficiently the oleaginous paste derived from the industrial processing of oil, both for animal feed and for direct human consumption, a field in which Mexico is still a beginner.

b) The Milk Industry

The shortage of milk production in Mexico, the need to provide milk as part of the population's minimum requirements and more importantly, to render it more accessible to the low-income classes, or at least to their children, has made it necessary to import large volumes over the medium and long term, apart from promoting the local milk industry. Transport and sanitary problems have lead to imports being brought from neighbouring countries. However, experience has shown that it is possible to overcome these obstacles by arranging package deals in which price, quality, transport and financing have all been considered.

Mexico must continue to develop industrialization techniques for rehydrating powdered milk or converting it into a form that can be more easily commercialized amongst the marginal urban and the rural population which normally does not have access to refrigeration. Another option would be to use powdered milk to enrich traditional foods, such

as flour and pasta, for example. It is in this field that European technology and capital can surely make a major contribution.

c) Animal Feed

Mexico is faced with the challenge of recovering and maintaining self-
sufficiency in a number of products for direct human consumption and
at the same time encouraging the production of different types of meat.
This has lead to the development of a major animal feed industry that is
highly dependent upon imported raw materials.

Among the projects aimed at reducing the deficit in this area and
diversifying supply sources is the development of yucca plantations in
tropical zones and the production of a unicellular protein from metha-
nol. In the latter field the United Kingdom leads the world in technology
and an interesting possibility would be for a consortium of companies or
European countries to develop production in Mexico so as to supply the
domestic market as well as to export. Mexico has elaborated a project
for producing 200 thousand tons of this protein.

A number of European countries have considerable experience in
growing yucca and in its use as animal feed as well as for human
consumption, due to their links with Africa. Also worth considering is
the broad scope offered in the utilization of farm by-products.

d) Fruit and Vegetables

The close proximity of the two nations implies that Mexico exports most
of its produce to the United States. However, there is clearly the need to
diversify the market for this most important part of Mexico's agriculture, a part that will continue to grow significantly. There is also the
immediate possibility of making better use of current production
through more efficient industrialization, as losses at present reach up to
30 percent.

The viability of exporting to European markets and counteracting the
effects of high transport costs lies in incorporating the highest added
value possible producing fruit and vegetable pastes, concentrates and
preserves. This would obviously require long-term programming and
pre-established contracts allowing produce to be selected and industrial
processes to maintain the quality required by the European markets.

Although the possibility of exporting fresh fruit and vegetables should
not be altogether discarded, past experience in this area has proved to be
unsatisfactory and it would need further progress to be made in preser-
vation and transport for this type of operation to be viable. Long-term
contracts could also help programme crops for this very same purpose.

e) Fish

Over the last few years Mexico has made major developments in tuna fishing and in the near future it could become a regular supplier to European markets of both frozen and processed tuna fish. More modern technology must be incorporated into processing this fish and at the same time new processes must be developed to reduce the high cost of conventional canning procedures, particularly from the point of view of the domestic market. A major fish processing plant is already under construction. The Mexican Government associated with a private French company which in turn had the financial support of its government with the granting of soft financing for the project. Part of the production will be for export.

In the past, some exports of whole prawns have been sent to Europe. This could represent a long-term prospect, perhaps even based on aquiculture production. Mexican fish production works in two main fields, large-scale fishing with nets and aquiculture in which there are some interesting possibilities for European participation. The number of boats needed for fishing surpasses current capacity to build or purchase. In many European countries there are a large number of boats that are virtually lying idle due to changes in fishing areas after the introduction of exclusive economic zones.

Mexico does not grant permission to foreign vessels to fish and it limits the use of foreign crew. However, we believe that formulas can be found for mutual cooperation in this field. On the other hand, aquiculture could be developed in Mexico with foreign participation and directed towards supplying the European market, for Mexican waters and climate provide very favourable conditions for the proliferation of many of the species commonly eaten in Europe, such as prawn, mussels, oysters, eel, etc. Once again, formulas will have to be developed to be able to form these associations and deal with Mexican legislation, which we feel can be done.

II. Mechanisms for Taking Action

Below is a brief review of the different mechanisms that may be of use in facilitating the above-mentioned possibilities of complementing food production. In order to overcome the traditional obstacles to greater interchange, not only commercial measures are required but also joint investment and technical and financial assistance, or a combination of policy with some of these additional measures.

a) Commercial Measures

Mexico's foreign trade in foodstuffs has mainly been directed towards the North American market for geographical, economic and technological reasons. Thus, the diversification of our trade requires a sustained effort on the part of all sectors together with government support. Another essential requisite is the same interest and support on the part of our possible business partners, in this case the European countries.

In some cases it will be necessary to undertake negotiations in which the principle of economic inequality must be taken into account. Barriers to primary commodities and manufactured goods must be reduced in order for these goods to compete in the European Common Market with those from countries that are nearer or that receive preferential treatment. In the same token, the possibility should be considered of bartering as a means of incorporating non-traditional exports and broadening our purchases from Europe. This could be applied by sectors or economic areas and could also include machinery and inputs for food production.

b) Joint-investment

The possibility of exporting food to Europe as well as importing it will be more feasible if Europe invests more in the Mexican food industry. The flow of capital would go hand in hand with the flow of raw materials and/or imputs and machinery, apart from the fact that the flow of trade generated would be more regular and durable. Joint-investment will also imply more solid and lasting technological links with Europe's industry.

c) Technical Assistance

In certain cases trade decisions or joint-investment may be undertaken more quickly depending on the technical assistance received from the respective governments. This mechanism has interesting potential in its application to specific projects. Furthermore, when foreign technology acquired in private ventures, the possibility of capitalizing the cost of this technology within the companies could be considered as a means a providing access to non-traditional sources of the same. These costs could also be covered with exports to the country or regions providing the technology.

d) Financial Cooperation

In order for the above-mentioned options to become a reality, it will depend in the long-term largely on Mexico's access to sources of financing appropriate to its current situation and heavy indebtedness. A very interesting case that has arisen lately has been Pescado de Chiapas, a large-scale industrial fishing project involving French capital, technology and equipment, and with the backing of very soft long-term credit granted by the French Treasury. This combination of private capital and foreign public financing in association with Mexican firms, in this case state-owned, could also be applied in other instances in the fishing industry and to agro-industry in general. New commercial trends could arise as a result and would tend to be directed towards participating countries.

If the EEC and its governing bodies, together with Mexico, can lend specific support to the concrete opportunities that arise and can exercise the flexibility needed to work out the combination of mechanisms required, then they will surely make steady progress towards a much greater and more varied economic interchange.

References

Centro de Estudios en Planeación Agropecuaria, El desarrollo agropecuario de México, pasado y perspectivas, Mexico, 1982

CEPAL, Economía campesina y agricultura empresarial. Tipología de productores del agro mexicano, Siglo XXI Editores, Mexico, 1982

De Alba, Francisco, Población, un sídrome de China in El desafío mexicano, Editorial Oceano, Mexico, 1982

Instituto de Investigaciones Económicas, UNAM, Fourth Seminar on Agricultural Economy in the Third World, Mexico, November 1984

Rafful, Fernando, Zonas deprimidas y política agrícola en México, MA thesis, Escuela Nacional de Economía, UNAM, Mexico, 1974

Shwedel, Kenneth, Structural Change and Policy in Mexican Agriculture Since 1965 (unpublished), Mexico, June 1985.

Appendix 1. Mexico's trade balance with the European Economic Communtiy. (FOB) (thousands of dallars)

Country	1979	1980	1981	1982	1983	January-September 1983	1984
Total							
Exports	511 521	1 124 380	1 629 058	2 590 047	2 185 799	1 648 708	2 057 546
Imports	2 013 982	2 549 886	3 227 304	2 222 203	1 216 596	835 436	932 236
Balance	−1 502 461	−1 425 506	−1 598 246	367 844	969 203	813 272	1 125 310
Belgium-Luxemburg							
Exports	69 525	77 277	66 065	67 257	57 574	36 470	66 397
Imports	113 159	154 730	123 591	81 052	47 338	37 576	64 023
Balance	−43 634	−77 453	−57 526	−13 795	10 236	−1 106	2 374
Denmark							
Exports	8 585	2 197	5 082	2 100	8 000	5 550	3 458
Imports	24 750	28 952	35 767	43 816	16 767	5 381	6 360
Balance	−16 165	−26 755	−30 685	−41 716	−8 767	169	−2 902
France							
Exports	71 686	566 781	931 298	931 066	821 223	608 664	715 814
Imports	500 239	520 438	621 289	349 336	370 752	220 614	205 189
Balance	−428 553	46 343	310 009	581 730	450 471	388 050	510 625
Ireland							
Exports	655	1 787	487	307	361	352	413
Imports	42 357	65 128	85 290	21 184	5 761	4 073	14 446
Balance	−41 702	−63 341	−84 803	−20 877	−5 400	−3 721	−14 033
Italy							
Exports	56 415	100 586	102 634	417 981	149 358	90 517	257 317
Imports	221 112	305 169	461 736	431 774	170 344	126 853	154 802
Balance	−164 697	−204 583	−359 102	−13 793	−20 986	−36 336	102 515

Netherlands							
Exports	46206	76295	65580	17931	33375	35941	30717
Imports	82227	98472	169979	103131	60939	48907	37095
Balance	—36021	—22177	—104399	—85200	—27564	—12966	—6378
United Kingdom							
Exports	45101	43503	244741	913051	855713	677924	802814
Imports	251187	405042	44774	278030	172865	108652	125618
Balance	—206086	—361539	—200033	635021	682848	569272	677196
West Germany							
Exports	213078	255954	213171	240354	260195	193290	180616
Imports	778951	971955	1284878	913880	371830	283380	324708
Balance	—565873	—716001	—1071707	—673526	—111635	—90090	—144092

Source: Banco Nacional de Comercio Exterior

Appendix 2. Mexico-European Economic Community trade balance for farm products (thousands of dollars)

	1980	1981	1982	1983
West Germany				
Exports	57288	45379	66246	78909
Imports	—	—	—	—
Balance	57288	45379	66246	78909
Belgium-Luxemburg				
Exports	—	12910	11369	13449
Imports	8969	10043	11802	8267
Balance	—8969	2867	—433	5182
France				
Exports	20018	15494	17755	10687
Imports	4601	10205	—	—
Balance	15417	5289	17755	10687
Ireland				
Exports	—	325	222	169
Imports	33990	65593	10961	1235
Balance	—33990	—65268	—10739	—1066
Italy				
Exports	24417	33180	10148	2140
Imports	—	—	—	—
Balance	24417	13180	10148	2140
Netherlands				
Exports	7250	5793	5078	2879
Imports	945	8049	5886	2243
Balance	6305	—2256	—808	636
United Kingdom				
Exports	20834	10506	4868	16539
Imports	21113	6405	—	—
Balance	—279	4101	4868	16539
Total				
Exports	129807	103587	115686	124772
Imports	69618	100295	28649	11745
Balance	60189	3292	87037	113027

Source: Instituto Mexicano de Comercio Exterior

Appendix 3. Mexico's major food product exports to European Economic Community member-countries (thousands of dollars)

	1980	1981	1982	1983
West Germany	*37214*	*33839*	*44258*	*70668*
Raw coffee beans (peeled)	25885	14127	29995	50475
Honey	11329	19712	14263	20193
Belgium-Luxemburg	—	*12633*	*6421*	*9518*
Raw coffee beans (peeled)	—	12633	6421	8893
Honey	—	—	—	625[1]
France	*20018*	*15157*	*15346*	*10214*
Raw coffee beans (peeled)	18669	12478	10803	5619
Asparagus without vinegar	1349	1759	3649	2456
Garlic	—	920	894	749
Beans	—	—	—	1390
Italy	*308*	*5207*	*3604*	*1480*
Frozen tuna fish	112	1931	1941	—
Raw coffee beans (peeled)	196	1268	—	—
Chick peas	—	2008	1663	999
Honey	—	—	—	481
Netherlands	*7250*	*4806*	*3958*	*1996*
Raw coffee beans (peeled)	3468	2758	921	1996
Liquid honey	3782	1279	—	—
Cocoa butter	—	769	2372	—
Cocoa beans	—	—	665	—
United Kingdom	*20834*	*10506*	*4868*	*16539*
Cocoa butter	—	—	1817	—
Lime essence	6328	1748	1778	3299
Asparagus without vinegar	2895	2394	804	3903
Honey	2736	1433	469	3533
Raw coffee beans (peeled)	8875	4931	—	—
Liquid honey	—	—	—	3332
Fermented cocoa beans	—	—	—	2472
Total	85624	82148	78455	110415

1. Figures taken from January to September
Source: Instituto Mexicano de Comercio Exterior

Appendix 4. Mexico's major food product imports from European Economic Community Member Countries (thousands of dollars)

	1980	1981	1982	1983
West Germany	—	—	—	—
Belgium–Luxemburg	*8969*	*10043*	*11802*	*8267*
Dehydrated butyric fats	8969	10043	11802	8267
France	*4601*	*10205*	—	—
Dehydrated butyric fats	4601	10205	—	—
Ireland	*33990*	*65593*	*10961*	*1235*
Milk powder	31365	54560	7450	—
Dehydrated butyric fats	2625	11033	3511	1235
Italy	—	—	—	—
Netherlands	*945*	*8049*	*5886*	*2243*
Dehydrated butyric fats	945	8049	5886	1233
Milk powder	—	—	—	1010
United Kingdom	*21113*	*6405*	—	—
Milk powder	21113	6405	—	—
Total	69618	100295	28649	11745

Source: Instituto Mexicano de Comercio Exterior

Cooperation between Mexico and the European Communities in the Energy Sector: Its Evolution and Some Hypotheses on Future Prospects

JORGE EDUARDO NAVARRETE

This paper discusses the evolution of cooperation between Mexico and the European Communities as regards energy together with some hypotheses on its future prospects. The work is intended to be an initial assessment of the subject and probably raises more questions than it can actually answer. It deals mainly with hydrocarbons, the predominant energy source, although mention is also made of other sources whose development could, with the help of the European Communities, well exceed its very limited quantitive importance in Mexico's energy balance and in that of the whole Latin American region. The paper does not attempt to gather exhaustive statistical information on the subject, although this information is available in a large number of Mexican, European and Latin American documents. But on the basis of this data the most important characteristics of the cooperation given to date are examined along with the direction this may take in the future. This text was designed more for discussion purposes than as an integrated part of this book. There is undoubtedly room for improvement.

Frame of Reference: Some Basic Features

During the late seventies, Europe saw in Mexico the oil supplier that could help reduce its dependence on supplies from the turbulent Middle East. Although situated on the other side of the Atlantic, there were many reasons why Mexico was considered the potentially most attractive partner in the developing world, from the point of view of both purchasing oil and doing business in the tranquil and optimistic atmosphere that pervaded the world economic scene during the last few years of the decade. Mexico had enjoyed prolonged political stability, interrupted only by transient disturbances like that of 1968, which did not appear to have left any permanent mark on the society. It had shown the capacity to come through the serious economic problems arising either from within or as a result of external events beyond its control, such as the crisis of 1976-77. There was the clear intention of the Mexican Government to accelerate oil extraction to a maximum and place as much crude oil as possible on the international market at a time when there was considerable uncertainty as to the availability of supply. Mexico had kept its distance from the OPEC and in fact appeared to be hostile to it when the organization established its hegemonic control over the international oil market. And finally, there was the prospect of prolonged prosperity, nurtured by the income from oil exports, which could easily have meant added oportunity for trade and investment.

There was a certain degree of concern as to Mexico's continued political stability, although it never really caused alarm. More so than in North America, Mexico's political system was admired, particularly because of the analysis done by the French politicologists, as a rare miracle of stability in a region characterized by sudden fluctuations between unstable civil governments and hard line military regimes. While there were no great illusions as to the effectiveness of conventional forms of democracy, the system was admired mainly because of its efficiency and continuity. What was important was that in Mexico, as opposed to other major or even intermediate Latin American countries, there would be no surprises. From the point of view of the Europeans, the reasons behind this were the Mexican's business. For them it was enough to know that stability would be maintained as it had been, for them to assume that there would be no real problems in the near future.

The economic situation, however, did cause more concern. The sudden end to over twenty years of monetary exchange stability and the inflationary explosion that occurred during the mid-seventies raised doubts as to the prudence with which Mexico's economic policy was being managed, particularly with the decision to substitute the "stabilizing development" model for an alternative one for which it is not easy to even find a name. When seen from the outside and especially from the other side of the ocean, the model that had produced the "Mexican miracle" did not encounter much objection and its substitution could not easily be explained, particularly if it was not successful. Nevertheless, oil had made its appearance providentially to save domestic economic policy from its own inefficiency and to reduce the losses arising from stagnant world economic activity and international trade during the mid-seventies. With the help of oil, recovery would soon be apparent.

Mexico's decision to accelerate to a maximum the exploration, extraction and export of crude oil was welcomed by a world avid for oil, particularly if it was to come from somewhere other than the Middle East. The promise of Mexican oil, more so than that from Alaska or the North Sea, lit up the sombre panorama of a world that was far too dependent on oil supplies from a very conflict-prone, unstable and unpredictable area. The excitement was even greater when it was realized that Mexico did not seem to be interested in cultivating its relations with other exporting countries, especially not those affiliated to the OPEC. Mexico intended to gain ground on them at any price, and that was exactly what it did from 1977 up until the time the market collapsed early in the present decade.

Mexico was determined to grow at any cost. Its population explosion had placed it under pressure, it had to overcome its backwardness, it considered itself a "middle power". It was interested in playing a more active role in international affairs and it was not going to let this unique opportunity pass by - it had to grow, and fast. Consequently, oil export earnings were converted into inputs, equipment and technological imports that grew at an unprecedented rate. In the insipid panorama of international trade during the late seventies, Mexico was one of the few bright stars. It purchased everything it was offered and was determined to carry out all its projects at the same time. When the income from oil became insufficient to finance the importing frenzy, the country resorted to foreign credit contracted under any conditions, with little heed to cost or terms. After all, credit for Mexico was apparently limitless. It was difficult to tell which was longer, the queue outside PEMEX's door wanting to buy oil or the one outside the treasury door offering credit. In Mexico this came to be known as "administering abundance".

Some of the major development projects that it was hoped would be financed with oil earnings and credit involved other branches of the energy sector, nuclear electricity in particular. The Plan Nacional de Energía (National Energy Plan) set itself some extremely ambitious objectives in this aspect. With the probable exception of Brazil and India, no other developing country had announced a programme for increasing nuclear electricity generation for the rest of the century. Overwhelmed by the cancellation or postponement of nuclear electricity projects in a fair number of industrialized countries, the suppliers of nuclear equipment, technology and materials in Europe and other areas saw Mexico as their golden opportunity. The plan also considered developing other energy sources, including the so-called new or renewable resources, with the aim of providing the country with a modern and diversified energy sector.

From Mexico's point of view, Europe was also particularly attractive. Afraid that its new oil wealth would only help strengthen its dependent relationship with the United States economy, Mexico showed a marked tendency to try and diversify its clientele abroad. As it had decided to increase its total export volume in as short a time as possible, it had to have alternative markets. The country depended on technology and inputs from abroad as well as foreign credit to be able to carry out its ambitious oil development program and Europe represented an important potential supplier of all of these. Mexico's intention, at least officially, was not to become an oil-based economy and it was determined to use its oil as a lever to develop other activities of consequence to international trade and economic cooperation. Europe provided the ideal environment for achieving these objectives.

Partly in response to historic circumstances and partly due to a long-term view of its future as an oil-exporting country, right from the beginning of its period as a major oil exporter, Mexico attempted to limit its dependence on its geographically closest market, a market at that time avid for additional supplies, although the most feasible means of achieving the proposed rapid growth in production and exports. The formula to achieve these objectives turned out to be a typically Mexican one - legislation - as if legal jurisdiction were capable of governing economic reality. The Plan Nacional de Energía (National Energy Plan) of 1979 established that no more than half of all exports could be sent to one single country. On the other hand, with the exception of Central America and the West Indies for whom preferential treatment was established jointly with Venezuela, sales to any given country could not exceed one fifth of the total imported by the same. The political reasoning behind these decisions was clearly explained by the Minister for Foreign Affairs early in 1980. "It is important", said Jorge Castañeda, "oil export earnings should not be too dependent on a single buyer, but it is even more important that the total requirements of any major importer should not depend on supplies from Mexico." In other words, the country did not want any one of its clients, particularly its closest neighbour, to develop an irreversable addiction to Mexican oil.

In its search for a more balanced and diversified export market, Mexico's efforts in promoting its exports were directed towards its most attractive options, i.e. Western Europe and Japan. In 1978, Mexico's first year as a major oil exporter, practically all its sales, i.e. 83.6 percent, were to oil companies in the United States. After two years this figure had been reduced to 60.6 percent. By 1982, the year of Mexico's economic disaster and the crisis in the international oil market, this share had fallen even more to reach 43.2 percent. Meanwhile, exports to Western Europe had gone from less than 5 percent in 1978, to 13.6 percent in 1980 and 15.2 percent in 1982.

These were years of frenzied searching on the part of the importers for oil supplies and Mexico logically decided to try and obtain additional advantages. Once more a legal formula inspired by the Foreign Office was introduced whereby "global agreements for bilateral economic cooperation" were established. The basic idea behind these agreements was to try and achieve mutual benefits for both parties in the bilateral economic relationship with industrialized buyer-countries, taking into account the contribution of each to the relationship and its respective level of development. Mexico participated mainly with supplies of oil as well as other products, a growing capacity to absorb inputs, equipment and technology and the opportunity for investment. The foreign parties were to contribute with the creation of easier access to their markets for Mexico's non-oil exports, particularly manufactured goods and by providing the equipment and technology necessary for the country's industrial modernization and diverisification, at competitive prices and under favourable conditions. They were also to provide financial support through credit and direct investment. The plan was initiated with several countries, including Spain and France in Europe, Canada in North America and Japan in the Far East. However, the crisis prevented these projects from coming to fruition.

Due to the crisis as well as other factors to be mentioned later on, things did not progress according to plan. Apart from one or two countries, Mexican oil did not play a very big part in Europe's scheme for importing crude oil. The drastic changes occurring in international oil market conditions after 1982 brought about a sudden reduction in the queues of potential buyers and money lenders at Mexico's doors. Oil supplies held less weight in the global plans for bilateral economic cooperation, while the need for deflationary adjustments put an end from one moment to the next to the importing boom. The development of export manufacturing fell foul of easy oil exports which had postponed the correction of Mexican industry's age-old bias against exporting. Economic contraction made investment opportunities much less attractive and Mexico's profound indebtedness brought about the withdrawal of voluntary credit from the commercial banking system as well as seriously affecting those export credits with an official guarantee. The nuclear electricity development programme was suspended *sine die* and

Mexico's intention to establish a modern and diversified energy sector was postponed indefinitely.

These constitute the basic features of the circumstances surrounding the attempts at cooperation in the energy field between Mexico and the European Communities after 1982 when the present administration took office.

Recent Evolution: Main Indicators

All in all, over the last few years Western Europe has been Mexico's second largest market for crude, its imports amounting to 364.5 thousand barrels per day (TBD) in 1983 as opposed to 823.2 TBD sent to the United States and 120.1 TBD to Japan. In 1984 the figures had changed to 409.9, 749.9 and 159.1 TBD, respectively. During the first few months of 1985 Western Europe purchased 359.5, the United States 753.0 and Japan 140.4 TBD. There is, however, very little diversification in Mexico's crude sales to Western Europe and during the last period mentioned, Spain, France and the United Kingdom absorbed over nine tenths of the total, with 45.3, 24.1 and 21.6 percent, respectively. The remaining nine percent was sent to Italy (5.6 percent), Portugal (1.9 percent) and Austria (1.5 percent). An interesting story lies behind these figures.

The ups and downs of crude oil exports obviously reflect the fluctuations that have been occurring in the world oil market over the last few years. However, they also reflect the fact that the European buyers of Mexican crude do not appear to be willing to enter into any long-term relationship while turning a blind eye to these fluctuations. Mexico is, in fact, just another supplier from whom one buys when it is convenient to do so in terms of current market conditions, and stops buying when its products become less competitive compared to other alternatives. This situation becomes quite clear if one observes the behaviour of oil exports to Europe during the first three quarters of 1985. During the first quarter, sales reached 437.0 TBD; during the second, when Mexico maintained its price levels despite generalized discounts on the part of other exporting countries, exports fell to less than half, i.e. 207.6 TBD; in the third, after a reduction in prices, exports rose again to 434.5 TBD. When Mexican oil became less competitive in the short-term, certain buyers, like Austria and Italy, stopped their purchasing completely, others like Spain and the United Kingdom cut them by half, while France reduced them to about a third.

This situation shows that Mexico has been unable to establish a stable relationship in oil trade with European buyers which would surpass the short-term fluctuations in the world market. It is clear that supplier diversification and the reduction in supplies from the Persian Gulf area have become less important for Europe in the light of the oil market glut that has existed since 1983.

The case of Spain deserves special mention not only due to its position as Europe's biggest importer of Mexican oil but also because it is the country with which Mexico has been able to establish a much more stable oil-related relationship, mainly through the participation of PEMEX capital in Petronor. By 1983, Mexico had established a solid exporting position with sales of 162,000 barrels per day, the second largest that year after the United States and equivalent to 20 percent of Spain's oil needs and 11 percent of Mexico's crude oil exports. Between 1980 and 1983 Mexican crude oil's share in Spain's oil imports had doubled. The relationship continued to evolve and in 1984 Spain was again Mexico's second largest buyer at 168,500 barrels per day, its relative importance remaining basically the same as regards the Spanish market and Mexico's total exports. During the first nine months of 1985 the volume exported was 162,850 barrels per day, the above-mentioned relative shares remaining constant. This positive evolution reflects the complementary objectives in Mexico's export policy and Spain's policy emphasizing diversification and sure supply.

In view of Spain's entry into the European Economic Community, a big change will occur in the Spanish oil sector's institutional regime, as part of the adjustment and industrial reconversion process that the incorporation into the EEC will require. Both parties must be prepared to face strong and growing competition. The changes in the oil sector will include eliminating foreign investment, with the exception of Mexico's share in Petronor, the formation of a company for transporting and distributing petroleum products and owned by the refining companies, the introduction of new crude purchasing policies on the part of the State, the liberalization of trade in petroleum derivates and the introduction of new mechanisms for determining the price of these products. These changes will have an adverse effect on Mexico's position as an exporter to Spain and will surely require adjustments to be made to Mexico's oil export policy to Spain. The basis for this policy must be continued complementary objectives. The Spanish Energy Programme gives priority to three factors related to crude supply, i.e. competitive prices and sure and diversified supply. Mexico's oil export policy satisfies these three requisites.

Mexico's cooperation with European nations in the field of energy is, of course, not limited to oil supply alone, although this is its most important aspect. Over the last few years there have been very noteworthy attempts at reaching an understanding on issues related to the international oil market with European oil exporting countries, Norway and the United Kingdom, and more recently there has been a positive response to an informal attempt on the part of Sweden, an importing country, to reactivate the global dialogue on the subject of energy.

As a player in the international oil scene, Mexico has tried since 1983 to maintain active and constant communication with other exporting countries both within and outside of the OPEC. The sole objective of this policy has been to collaborate in the stabilization and eventual recovery of the market. For this reason Mexico has occasionally assisted as a formal observer at ministerial conferences and other important meetings of the Organization, and the Mexican oil authorities have often visited both London and Oslo. Contact has also been maintained with the International Energy Agency in Paris. These contacts have allowed major differences in attitudes and points of view to be brought to light. Unlike the European exporters, Mexico feels that the only possible way of defending international oil prices, at least while present market conditions persist, is to control supply. It is obvious that this idea is not shared by the countries of the North Sea which in general have continued to increase their production to a maximum and it appears to be their intention to continue doing so. There is here a basic difference between the two points of view. While Mexico considers that the oil market should continue to be governed by a system of controlled prices, as has traditionally been the case, Norway and the United Kingdom are inclined more towards free market operations. It would appear that the events of the past months are an indication of the collapse of the controlled price system administered by the OPEC. However, in the long run, if sudden repeated fluctuations in oil prices are to be avoided, this system will have to be replaced with another in which importers will also have to participate in the interests of market stability and predictability.

It was this type of consideration that lead Mexico to respond positively in 1984 to the Swedish Government's initiative aimed at determining whether or not a sufficiently favourable international environment existed to be able to reopen an informal dialogue between both exporters and importers of oil, for the purpose of defining possible courses of action designed to reestablish stability and promote oil market recovery. Unfortunately, the number of positive responses was small and Sweden abandoned the project. It is obvious that amongst the majority of the market participants, especially the consumers, there is considerable short-sightedness and lack of concern as to what may happen during the next decade or even later on. It is not easy to condone this attitude.

Several very definite instances of cooperation have been undertaken between Mexico and the European Community over the last few years in the energy sector. Most of them were decided upon at the Mixed Commission for Economic Cooperation between Mexico and the Community, which held its fifth meeting in December 1984 and is about to hold its sixth one in Brussels early in November this year. Most of these activities involve technical cooperation and are related to nuclear energy and new and renewable sources. It can be seen that Europe has continued to observe the long-term development in Mexico's energy sector and is interested in the possibility of participating with equipment, technology and materials.

The minutes of the meeting of the Mixed Commission for Economic Cooperation between Mexico and the European Community in December 1984 records "satisfaction for the progress made in energy cooperation" towards which the Ministry for Energy, Mines and State-owned Industry, the Institute for Electrical Research and El Colegio de Mexico amongst other institutions have contributed on the part of Mexico. Also recorded here is the sum of 1.1 million ECUs for the development of specific projects in the energy sector for 1985.

Amongst the projects of particular interest is that related to geothermal power and for which a seminar will be arranged for mid-1986 on the development and exploitation of geothermal resources, organized in conjunction with the Institute for Electrical Research (IER). Another project is being undertaken with the Ministry for Energy, Mines and State-owned Industry whereby a computer model will be installed for the supply and utilization of energy. Of particular importance are certain technological projects established between Electricité de France and the IER related to the generation and distribution of electric energy and worker capacitation.

Future Prospects for Cooperation: Some Hypotheses

During the rest of this decade and probably for an even longer period to come, oil supply will continue to be the main component of Mexican-European cooperation in the field of energy. Its future will therefore depend upon the evolution of the international oil market at present somewhat uncertain.

The future behaviour of the OPEC countries and the consequences this will have on market stability are unsure. Also an unknown factor is the behaviour of other exporters in North America and Europe, non-members of the OPEC, who appear to be unconcerned about the repercussions their policies and actions might have on the market. Also equally uncertain is the evolution of future demand on the part of the consumers, as well as the way in which the different energy sources are combined in the organization of each country's energy balance and the changes occurring in the relationship between economic growth and energy consumption. The attitudes of the large transnational oil corporations are also difficult to foresee, as are all the possible political reactions that a given combination of attitudes and actions on the part of the main actors could have on the oil market, world economy and international relations.

Despite these uncertainties, no-one can deny that it is in the interests of all the participants in the international oil market to promote order and predictability in the same. However, until real discipline is reestablished in the OPEC members' trading behaviour and ample collaboration achieved with non-OPEC exporters, and whilst effective dialogue and communication is not established between producers and consumers, this somewhat ambitious objective will never be feasible.

In the long run, the institutional structure of the oil market will undoubtedly have to evolve from the prevailing "Brotherhood associations", such as the OPEC versus the AIE, to a more cooperative, less conflictive system where all concerned can make their common interests known and work together to achieve them.

As far as its relationship with buyer-countries in Europe, it seems very unlikely that Mexico will be able to achieve in the near future the conditions necessary to establish stable long-term supply irrespective of daily market fluctuations. Nevertheless, the uncertainty pervading the situation as a whole does not exclude the possibility of unexpected changes of fortune. One cannot discard the possibility that in the future it may once more be important to be able to count on a sure supply of oil from non-conflictive areas. Prices could still fluctuate sharply and there is still the possibility of an oil shortage as there was from 1979-1980. Thus, it would be advisable for more workable oil trade relations to be cultivated between Mexico and Europe. Amongst the measures worth considering could be the establishing of basic levels of supply, obligatory for all parties concerned, complementing supply with participation in refining or even distribution activities, diversifying the range of products included in the interchange and moving more and more towards the use of LPG and other derivates. The idea is to create a lasting economic relationship whose long-term evolution is of importance to each party.

Dialogue and communication must be maintained with exporters from Western Europe. The objective is obviously not to convince them to adopt Mexico's point of view, nor that Mexico adopts that prevailing among the North Sea countries. The aim is rather that each have information available to them on the policies and actions of the other, that each party understand more clearly the reactions that their own measures may have on the other and that there be an interchange of information on the way in which each one sees the future of the market. At some stage this interchange could bring about joint activities in the field of trade and technological cooperation, among others.

It would also be worthwhile promoting cooperation in other areas of the energy sector aside from oil. Nuclear electricity is a particularly promising field. Although Mexico's nuclear electric development programmes will probably not be reactivated on a large scale at least until the 1990s, it is clearly in the interests of the country to keep its options open as regards diversification and consider some of the possible alternatives offered by some European countries. Sustained cooperation in the field of technological research will pave the way for later development. In the same token, this can be applied to activities related to new or renewable energy sources, particularly solar energy and geothermal power.

Thus, by placing Mexican oil and petroleum products on the European Community markets under more stable and lasting conditions, creating a more systematic dialogue with European oil exporters on the future prospects for the international market and undertaking pertinent activities involving technological cooperation in alternative energy sources, particularly nuclear electricity, the foundations will have been laid for achieving real progress in Mexican-European cooperation efforts in the energy sector. Later on in the next decade, the reactivation of energy diversification projects in Mexico will help pave the way for even broader cooperation in benefit of both parties.

PART 6

THE SECOND ENLARGEMENT

The Impact of the Second Enlargement of the European Community on Latin American Economies

ALFRED TOVIAS

The aim of this paper is straightforward. First and foremost one must draw an exact picture of the institutional links between Latin American countries, the European Community and its new member countries both before and after the Enlargement has taken place. This allows in a second part of the paper to compare the two situations and predict the direct trade effects derived from the changes in the institutional setting. This in turn allows for a qualitative evaluation of static welfare effects, as well as of other often neglected effects. As a way of conclusion, present and future Spanish policies regarding the implications of the Enlargement for Latin America are reviewed and evaluated.

Institutional Changes and a priori Impact on Latin American Trade Flows

From an analytical perspective, the pre-Enlargement situation is as follows:

1. *EC-Latin American institutional links* consist of:
    a. a series of bilateral cooperation agreements involving the concession by the two sides of most-favoured nation (i.e. non-preferential) treatment between the Community and several Latin American countries (Brazil, Mexico, Uruguay, Andean Group). Since most of the latter are GATT members anyway, the agreements do not have practical value.
    b. a series of bilateral agreements on textiles between on the one hand the EC and on the other hand Brazil, Columbia, Guatamala, Haiti, Mexico, Peru, Uruguay involving voluntary export restrictions by the Latin American partner. Note that because Argentina has refused to

conclude "voluntarily" to such an agreement, the EC has imposed unilaterally restrictions on textile imports originating from that country.

c.   two bilateral agreements on sheep and lamb meat between the EC and both Argentina and Uruguay involving voluntary export restrictions by the Latin American partner.

d.   an agreement between the EC and Brazil on manioc whereby the EC opens annual tariff quotas in favour of imports from Brazil.

2. *Latin American countries* benefit since 1971 from GSP treatment in the European Community, along with all other Third World countries, on those items covered by the scheme and provided they respect all the conditions imposed by the Community. Moreover, since GSP treatment is unilaterally conceded it can be withdrawn at short notice.

3. *Spanish-EC institutional links* are governed by the June 1970 Preferential Agreement which in practical terms, breaks down as follows:

a.   a partial Preferential Agreement for industrial products including:

– a 60% reduction of the Common External Tariff (CET) on most industrial imports originating in Spain
– a 40% reduction of the CET for a restricted list of products including salt, tires, woolens, synthetic fibres, stockings, undergarments, shoes, lead and zinc
– no CET reduction on various other goods including coal and steel products, foodstuffs (sugar, chocolate, etc.), certain textile fibres, cork and cork by-products.
– preferential tariff quotas on Spanish refined petroleum products, some cotton fabrics and raisins.
– a 25% reduction on most industrial imports from the EC
– a 60% reduction of the Spanish tariff on a few industrial products for which the most favoured nation rate is generally low in any case.
– no reduction of Spanish tariffs on a large number of products, including coal and steel products, paper, silk, cotton, electrical machines and appliances, boilers, watchers, plastic materials and fertilizers.

b.   partial tariff preferences on a number of Spanish agricultural exports (including food products) comprising a 30% to 50% reduction of the CET, but none at all on other agricultural products (comprising about 35% of Spanish agricultural exports).

c.   partial tariff preferences on EC agricultural exports, with reductions in the Spanish tariff generally reaching 60% (including living cattle beef).

4. *Spanish-EFTA institutional links* are dominated by the Agreement of 26 June 1979 (implemented as of May 1, 1980), which provides for:

    a.   A fully-implemented Preferential Trade Agreement for industrial products with conditions *identical* to those prevailing between Spain and the EC.

    b.   fully-implemented bilateral agreements between Spain and individual EFTA countries (Austria, Finland, Norway, Portugal, Sweden and Switzerland) covering trade in agricultural products. In most such agreements, Spain obtains tariff preferences on EFTA imports from Spain. Some of them overlap with products exported by Latin American countries (like fish, citrus fruit, coffee, spices, cocoa, flowers).

5. *Spanish-EC Agreement on Textiles,* according to which the EC was allowed to institute a surveillance system on Spanish exports of textile products to the EC from 1978 on. In 1979, a system of administrative cooperation between the parties was introduced. A more restrictive agreement is in force regarding steel products.

6. *Portuguese-EC institutional links* are governed by the 1972 Agreement providing for:
- free trade in industrial products. The agreement has been fully implemented insofar as Portugal's exports to the EC are concerned, although not in the reverse direction. Full tariff liberalization on Portugal's part has been linked to the outcome of negotiations for accession to the EC (see later).
- preferential tariff reductions on Portuguese agricultural exports to the EC.

7. *A Portuguese-EC Agreement on Textiles*, following the Spanish-EC pattern (see paragraph 5 above).

8. *Greek-EC institutional links* are governed by the 1979 Accession Treaty, according to which Greece was to enter the EC as of January 1, 1981. As the period of transition to full implementation (ending 1986-1988, according to products) is not yet over, one can focus on one of two pre-Enlargement situations: the present one (late 1985) or that which prevailed as of 31 December 1980. In the opinion of this author the second option corresponds more closely to the concept of "pre-Enlarge-

ment". At that time, institutional links were governed by the 1961 Greece-EC Association Agreement, which provided for free trade in industrial products and partial tariff preferences on agricultural products. The Agreement was fully implemented as far as Greece's industrial exports to the EC were concerned, with certain minor exceptions (see below). On the other hand, the free trade stage for Greece's industrial imports had not been attained. Moreover, a Greek-EC Agreement on Textiles imposed QRs on Greek's textiles exports to the EC.

The assumed *post-Enlargement* situation may be described as follows:

1.* *EC-Latin American institutional links* are assumed to remain essentially the same, except for the following changes: Greece, Spain and Portugal become a party to all the bilateral agreements mentioned under 1a), 1b), 1c) and 1d). As mentioned in 1) above, adopting 1a) is of no practical consequence. Of course, in the medium or the long run, the EC may decide to review seriously its relationship with Latin America under pressure from Spain (see later), but this cannot be considered as a direct outcome of the Enlargement *per se*.

2.* *Latin American countries* benefit, after a transition period, of GSP treatment also in the three new member countries. For example, according to the Spanish Accession Treaty, Spain shall progressively apply the Generalized Preference System starting on March 1, 1986. Observe that the duties applied as from that date are identical to those applied *on EC-originating* imports. This rule does not apply however to 51 products for which duties taken initially for gradual dismantling are those effectively applied *by Spain* before the Enlargement on imports originating from GSP countries. The preferential rates applied by the Community nowadays will only take effect for most goods by January 1, 1996, with the important exception of fish products, for which the relevant date is January 1, 1993.

3.* *Spanish-EC post-Enlargement status* is governed by the EC Accession Treaty signed on June 12, 1985. Applying the same line of reasoning employed for pre-Enlargement in the Greek case (see above), two periods may be considered: the date the Agreement first becomes valid (January 1, 1986) or the time that all its provisions are implemented (by January 1, 1996). The second option more closely corresponds to the concept of post-Enlargement, i.e., a situation wherein all effects of the

Accession Treaty have taken place, rather than one characterized by juridical implications alone.

According to these assumptions, the post-Enlargement situation could be described as follows:

a.   free trade in industrial products between Spain and the EC (to be fully implemented by January 1, 1993);

b.   free trade in agricultural products between the two sides to be fully implemented by January 1, 1996 for most goods. Note, however, that the deadline is already 1993 for beef and veal (of interest to Latin American countries);

c.   Spain applies the CET (by January 1, 1993)[1];

d.   Spain adopts the 1972 EC agreements with individual EFTA countries, implying free trade in industrial products and possibly the obtaining of further agricultural concessions from EFTA members[2];

e.   Spain becomes a party to the Lomé Convention III[3];

f.   Spain becomes a party to all individual agreements between the EC and Mediterranean countries[4];

g.   Spain joins the EC scheme of tariff preferences on exports of developing countries, including those in Latin America (See above). The alignment of Spanish tariffs on the EC's preferential rate is made progressively from March 1, 1986 through January 1, 1993 for manufactured goods and fish products and through January 1, 1996 for agricultural exports;

h.   suppression of surveillance measures on Spain's textile exports to the EC (to be implemented by January 1, 1990);

i.   free trade in industrial and agricultural goods between Spain and Portugal (to be implemented by 1990);

j.   Spain adopts the EC restrictive agreements on textiles and on lamb and sheep meat imports (from Argentina and Uruguay).

k.   Spain adopts the Common Agricultural Policy (CAP).

A number of other items are *not* relevant to this study (e.g. movements of capital) and will be ignored in what follows.

4.*   *Spain declares* unilaterally in its Accession Treaty that "...in order to avoid sudden disturbances in its imports originating in Latin America, (it) has highlighted in the negotiations the problems which arise from the application of the "acquis communautaire" to certain products. Partial and temporary solutions have been adopted for tobacco, cocoa and coffee". Moreover "Spain...proposes finding permanent solutions in the context of the Generalized System of Preferences, when next revised, or of other mechanisms existing within the Community".

5.* *Portuguese-EC post-Enlargement* status will be governed by the Accession Treaty of June 12, 1985. Again as in the case of Spain, the focus is laid upon the post-transition period situation - whenever it differs from the current one - characterized by:
- the elimination of remaining Portuguese preferential tariffs on EC and EFTA industrial exports;
- other changes, identical with items b-k (excluding d) listed for Spain (see 3* above).

6.* *Greek-EC post-Enlargement* status, as indicated above, will have been attained by 1988 upon the full implementation of the 1979 Greek-EC Accession Treaty. Note that this stage will differ from the afore-mentioned pre-Enlargement situation as follows:
- elimination of remaining Greek-preferential tariffs on EC industrial exports;
- all other changes (excepting item a) listed for Spain (see above 3*).

7.* A *"Joint Declaration of Intent"* on the development and intensification of relations with the countries of Latin America is adopted by the Community, Spain and Portugal and annexed to the Final Act concerning the conditions of accession and the adjustments to the Treaties signed on June 12, 1985. In it, the Community "reaffirms its resolve to extend and strengthen its economic, commercial and cooperation relations with (Latin American) countries" and is prepared to step up the level of relationships, taking into account "the scope of the generalized system of preferences and the application of the economic cooperation agreements concluded or to be concluded with certain Latin American countries or groups of countries".

Finally, Spain is assumed to suspend her participation in the 1971 Protocol of Trade Negotiations among Developing Countries - to which Brazil, Chile, Mexico, Peru, Uruguay and Paraguay are parties as well - which involves the concession of reciprocal tariff preferences on a bilateral basis among the signatories to the Protocol.[5]

It is thus evident that "Operation Enlargement" is rather complex. This, however, does not justify the practice of focussing upon selected changes and totally ignoring others, as reflected in numerous studies published to date.[6]

A second obvious preliminary conclusion is that the impact upon Latin American economies of the entry of each of the three Mediterranean countries into the EC (thereinafter "the Three") will differ because their pre-Enlargement institutional links with the Community were by no means identical. Note that this is true independently of the other differentiating variables so frequently mentioned in the literature (such as the Three's respective economic dimensions, the extent of their trade's overlap with third countries' imports, and so on).

Schematically, the most relevant changes for Latin American countries are the following:

1.   Spain will obtain free access to the EC for its agricultural exports, improving its status of preferred Mediterranean country, which entails very few tariff reductions at present. The same is essentially true for Portugal, although not significantly so for Greece, whose agricultural exports were mostly exempted from tariff duties even *before* its accession.

2.   The Community obtains free access into Spanish, Greek and Portuguese agricultural markets.

3.   The Three will join the CAP upon accession to the EC, with all the advantages that this implies (e.g. export refunds, guaranteed prices, and so on) reaching them progressively after transition periods. They will also have to respect after a while certain common disciplines (corresponsibility prices, some production restraints, quality requirements, etc.) and apply the principle of Community preference and common agricultural prices.

4.   The Three must adopt the EC's CET. This invariably implies a reduction in tariff protection levels on non EC countries' industrial exports, although not so for some agricultural commodities (e.g. coffee).

5.   Spain, on the one hand and the EC and EFTA on the other hand will increase their margins of preference on mutual industrial trade to 100%, thereby attaining a level of free trade in industrial goods. *A priori*, there are two reasons why the change appears to be much more significant for Spain's industrial imports from the EC and EFTA than for those of the EC or EFTA originating in Spain:

– Spain's tariffs are generally much higher than those of the EC.
– Present Spanish tariff preferences on EC and EFTA products are much lower than EC or EFTA preferences for Spanish products.

A second glance at the situation leads to a slight reassesment: the EC and EFTA will have to eliminate after the transition period their highly restrictive limitations on "sensitive" products originating in Spain, including textiles and steel products. Note that the change in the industrial field is much more significant for Spain than for Greece and Portugal, as the latter benefited from free access to the EC (except for textile trade) even before the Enlargement and offered the EC a wider access to their markets than did Spain (through implementation of the 1961 Association Agreement with Greece and the 1972 Free Trade Agreement with Portugal.[7]

6.   The Three will get tariff-free access for their industrial exports and preferential status for their agricultural exports in the Israeli market. Also, tariff preferences will be applied on their exports to Cyprus, Malta and Turkey.

7.   All Mediterranean and ACP countries will have free access without any limitations for their industrial exports into the Spanish, Portuguese and Greek markets. GSP (including Latin American) countries get also tariff-free treatment in those markets but with limitations. Observe that the proportional tariff reduction for imports originating from these countries is much larger than for those from the EC or EFTA since the starting tariff applied by the Three was already lower in the latter case.[8]

8.   ACP countries' agricultural exports get free access into the Three's markets. Moreover the latter's agricultural imports originating in Mediterranean countries will benefit from partial tariff preferences (on a much wider scale than under the GSP scheme).

9.   The Three must adopt the EC Textile agreements with several Latin American countries, as well as those dealing with sheep and lamb meat.

10.   Spain, as Greece did before, must withdraw from a scheme of trade preferences among developing countries, which includes six Latin American countries.

Direct Trade Effects

Table 1 sums up the aforementioned changes and their *a priori* impact upon Latin American countries. In general, four types of effects have been distinguished (from a Latin American perspective): trade creation; trade diversion against Latin American exports; trade diversion in favour of Latin American exports and against other countries (belonging to the developed world or to the Eastern bloc); and trade destruction. This terminology is used in the theory of Customs Unions as developed by Viner, Lipsey and Meade.

Table 1 indicates the following facts:

a. Previous studies on the impact of the Second Enlargement upon Latin American countries have focused almost exclusively upon lines 1,2,7 and 8 for several reasons[9]:

– From a quantitative viewpoint, these effects may dominate all others. However, this is not a sufficient reason to ignore the latter outright.
– The quantification of some effects (e.g. lines 3,4 and 9) may be hazardous or premature until the exact conditions set in the Accession Treaties are known.
– There is some widespread ignorance of what the acceptance of the "Acquis communautaire" by the Three implies. For instance, no previous study on the present subject[10] mentions the fact that the Three get easy (if not free) access into EFTA, Israeli or Turkish markets for most products, including some food exports of interest to Latin American countries (e.g. rice, vegetable oil, fish products, flowers); or identically, but in the reverse direction Israeli cotton or Turkey's tobacco exports to Spain and Portugal (see lines 5,6 and 8).
– Studies, particularly if government-initiated, tend to stress the effects which harm the non-candidate's exports and in light of which, and at the same time, it may expect some meaningful concession or compensation from the EC, as discrimination is indeed in evidence. This last point requires some elaboration: research focussing on Latin American problems with the Enlargement have placed little emphasis upon line 5, because Latin America already got free access to EC or EFTA industrial markets through application of GSP schemes, while Spain, Greece and Portugal (the latter two for textiles) do not as long as the Enlargement does not take place. Hence there is little which Latin American countries can request as compensation in the industrial field, apart from asking for the revision of the Textile Agreements or a further improvement of the GSP scheme (coverage, limitations, butoirs, etc.).[11] This however, does not imply that actual trade diversion on these items will be insignificant[12]; logically, therefore, these effects should deserve considerable attention.

b. Relating to the negative effects (shown in lines 1, 3 and 5a) taken together, one can assert that in general not only quantities exported by non members tend to drop but also prices charged must be lowered in relation to the pre-Enlargement situation, whenever the domestic price in the EC drops as a result of the Three's entry into the Community. The future looks awkward for products overlapping with Spanish exports (vegetables, olive oil, citrus fruit, wood products, steel products, footwear, leather products), less so regarding Portugal and Greece (e.g. tobacco), as duties on their agricultural exports and most industrial

Table 1. General and sectoral trade creation (t.c.), trade diversion (t.d.) and trade destruction (t.des.) affecting Latin American trade with the EC as a result of Enlargement

Changes in new members' trade links with the EC	A Greece	B Portugal	C Spain
1) Free access to EC agricultural markets	—	g.t.d.	g.t.d.
2) Free acceptance of EC agricultural goods	g.t.d.	g.t.d.	g.t.d.
3) Joining the CAP	g.t.d.	g.t.d.	g.t.d.
4) Adopting the CET a)on industrial imports	g.t.c.	g.t.c.	g.t.c.
b)on agricultural imports	t.des.	t.des.	t.des.
5) a)Free access to EC and EFTA industrial markets	g.t.d. to EFTA × textile t.d. to EC	textile t.d.	g.t.d. to EC and EFTA
b)Free acceptance of EC and EFTA industrial goods	g.t.c.	g.t.c.	g.t.c.
6) Free or facilitated access to some Mediterranean markets	g.t.d.	g.t.d.	g.t.d.
7) Free acceptance of Mediterr. +ACP and developing c. industrial imports	g.t.c. + t.d. in favor of partner	g.t.c. + t.d. in favor of partner	g.t.c. + t.d. in favor of partner
8) Free or easier acc. of ACP/Med. agr. prod. into Three's markets	g.t.d.[9]	g.t.d.[9]	g.t.d.[9]
9) Adopting EC's Textile Agreements	g.t.d.	g.t.d.	g.t.d.
10) Withdrawing from 1971 Protocol	g.t.d.	---	g.t.d.

products were nil even before Enlargement. The only advantage they would now receive are benefits obtained under the CAP (like penetration primes, which are to be probably eliminated in the future) and last but not least, free access for their textiles. The question of the effect of these changes upon world prices is all too frequently neglected, because of the assumption that neither the EC is an important consumer in world markets nor the Three are key world-wide suppliers. This is, however, not the case at least for several fruits and vegetables, and olive oil. For example, trade diversion in favour of Spain and Greece could reach proportions large enough to lower world citrus prices. In such an eventuality, Brazil would have to bear the impact of Enlargement in her exports to the United States or Canada. Moreover, should trade diversion be more than total, i.e. if non-members countries' exports are kept out of EC markets and the Three are left with domestic surpluses, the latter would benefit from export restitutions under the CAP. Those subsidized exports to non-EC countries would then further reduce world prices.[13]

c.   The changes noted in lines 4a) and 5b) lead to trade creation favoring Latin American countries. By opening their markets fully to the EC and EFTA and improving access for other developed countries, the new members will increase their import demand for final goods, thus increasing, in turn, third-party countries' demand for Latin American intermediary products.[14] This of course will occur quite independently of the fact that direct industrial exports to the Three are expected to undergo an overall increase at both the final and intermediary goods levels because of introduction of the GSP by the Three (see line 7). Note, however, that in some cases, Spain and Greece are replacing one kind of preferential treatment regarding Latin American imports (see line 9) for another. Observe also that, because of the two countries's withdrawal from the 1971 Protocol of Trade Negotiations among Developing Countries, some Spanish and Greek exports to Latin American countries may be diverted to other destinations, over and above the expected export trade deversion derived from the creation of a Free Trade Area between the Three and the rest of Western Europe. To sum up, Latin American industrial exports *to the Three*, with the exception of textiles and processed food, should increase as a consequence of the Enlargement, whether direct or indirect. A geometrical analysis would show that Latin American countries can divert exports, sold previously at world prices, to the Three, where they will fetch a higher price, dictated by Community and EFTA export supply prices (assumed to be in many instances over and above Japanese or US prices). But most important of all there may be net export expansion, because the higher prices allow for some production at higher costs. In other words, for Latin America, the Enlargement implies the addition of three markets with a GNP (in 1983) slightly higher than that of Benelux countries, to which it can export at privileged prices. The higher the difference is between average European and world prices, the higher the expected impact. This is particularly true for sensitive products such as footwear, steel, automobiles, shipbuilding.

d.   Finally, one must relate to Latin American agricultural exports to the Three. Consider *simultaneously* lines 2, 3, 4b and 8 and the expected outcome becomes crystal-clear: Latin American exports should drop at least on four accounts. Not only that the CET is higher than the present level of protection afforded to local produce in the Three for many basic commodities (e.g. coffee), but also that barriers on competing EC products are going to disappear (e.g. veal and beef, cereals). Add to this, that Mediterranean and ACP countries get privileged access (e.g. coffee imports from ACP countries are tariff-free) and the picture becomes totally bleak. Add to it that variable levies provided for by the CAP represent an additional protection on top of the CET which on average is at least three times higher than the latter. Sampson and Yeats (1980) have calculated the nominal and effective rates for many products. Some of them are exported by Latin American countries to Spain or Portugal nowadays, facing low barriers. Hereunder are given three examples:

Table 2.

Description	Nominal rate (%)		Effective rate (%)	
	Tariffs	Levies	Tariffs	Levies
Wheat	20.0	73.0	40.6	154.1
Maize	6.0	34.1	10.7	72.0
Bovine meat	20.0	64.2	38.2	215.2

Source: Sampson and Yeats (1980)

Other products exported by Latin America to the Three which will be hit by the Enlargement are corn, oil seeds, sugar. The situation confronted by Latin America in this respect is similar to the one of non-ACP Commonwealth countries after the accession of the United Kingdom into the EC. It was this precedent in relation to arrangements for New Zealand that was invoked by Spanish officials during negotiations for accession, but without success. One reason may have been that Spain could not prove having as close a relationship with Latin America as Britain could in relation to the Commonwealth.

Static Welfare Effects

The above analysis clearly indicates that positive welfare effects are concentrated on the exporter's side. Latin American consumers are most probably not going to benefit from lower prices after the Enlargement, but for a few quite marginal cases (see below) some prices may even go up (see line 10).

Exporters may be divided into three categories, according to whether they are hurt by the Enlargement, benefit therefrom or remain unaffected. Latin American countries are obviously concerned about the first group, which primarily comprises the agricultural community as well as some light industries. The impact upon welfare results from a drop in the average export price to all destinations not only to the Twelve. That is, world prices will also be affected, as some EC agricultural surplus production will be dumped in world markets, given export restitutions offered to EC agricultural producers according to CAP rules.

The negative welfare impact on Latin American industrial exporters appears more limited; apparently, as noted earlier, no systematic drop in the EC or EFTA domestic prices is to be expected after Enlargement. This could occur, however, for categories of EC imports whose access was highly restricted to the three new member countries prior to the Enlargement, including textiles, clothing, steel products, refined petroleum products, footwear and cork products. As indicated above, the Three will be accorded free access not only into the EC, but also into EFTA, a situation differing from that which applies to agricultural products. This is highly relevant for "sensitive products" *not* covered by the GSP schemes of EFTA countries.

Latin American exports which should benefit from the Enlargement include not only industrial products already marketed to the three new member countries (such as chemical products or some transport equipment), but also those which were previously not sold there at all because of high tariffs and preference for EC and EFTA products in those markets (e.g. machinery). Spain and Greece are among the most developed NICs with a per capita GNP four times higher than the average Latin American country and similar, if not higher, than Ireland (a member of the EC), only marginally smaller than that of Italy and are not substantially inferior to that of the United Kingdom.

Increased Price Instability in World Agricultural Markets of Interest to Latin American Countries

Theoretical analysis has shown that the introduction of the EC's CAP in the 1960s not only depressed world agricultural prices, but also increased the rate of price instability. Sampson and Snape (1980) demonstrate that the introduction of a variable levies system allows for local market instability to be shifted to the rest of the world. Not all products exported by Latin America to the EC or the Three are covered by the system. However, reinforcement of the Mediterranean farmers' lobby in the Enlarged EC and the pressure exerted by French wine and fruit producers hit by the Enlargement to be compensated somehow by the Community is expected to bring about inclusion of many new agricultural products in the system (e.g. flowers). The rate of price instability itself (and not only the coverage of products) will increase, as some of the former price instability was absorbed by the new member countries, which were competing with Latin America not only in the EC but in world markets as well (e.g. citrus fruit, tobacco, cotton, vegetables, rice, flowers). Moreover, if Spain becomes an agricultural superpower in fruit and vegetables, as many have anticipated, any annual or seasonal change in her supply conditions will have a higher incidence upon world market prices than it does at present. While neo-classical economists do not tend to attach much significance to the welfare effects of price instability in world markets, one can recall nonetheless that an increased level would exacerbate the overall uncertainty facing the Latin American exporter. Farming will become an increasingly risky activity. After all, Latin American countries were among the most active in the discussion held in UNCTAD for the establishment of the Common Fund and of an Integrated Program for Commodities.

Investment Diversion in Favour of the Three New Member Countries

There is a fairly large economies of scale potential in many Spanish and Portuguese industries (including the manufacture of paper, rubber tires, chemicals and machinery).[15] Free access to the EC coupled with higher availability of lower-priced credit funds (through further opening of credit and money markets) may lead to optimum scale specialization in branches such as automobiles, railway equipment and electrical engineering.[16] The same can be said of agriculture, wherein scale economies have not been fully exploited for lack of markets and/or cheap credit. Moreover, as B. Balassa has often stressed, accession to the EC (and its Customs Union) reduces the level of uncertainty attached to any export transaction with other members of the Community, as the irrevocable reduction of trade barriers becomes an incentive to export-oriented investment. On the other hand, GSP treatment may be revoked unilaterally at short notice, something that must be entered into the equation when evaluating long-term investment risks. Therefore, the Enlargement could draw potential investments from Latin American NICs (e.g. Brazil, Argentina, Colombia) towards Spain, Greece or Portugal which, as members of the EC, would be perceived as less likely to lose their privileges therein.

EC Aid and Cooperation Policies

Upon Enlargement, Latin American countries' prospects of maintaining or enlarging their credit or grant aid envelopes could be hampered for at least two reasons:

1. The net cost of the Enlargement will exert new pressures on the EC budget. Not only must the supplementary costs of sustaining agricultural markets be taken into account, but also of restructuring aid to the Mediterranean regions of the EC (Mediterranean Integrated Programmes).

2. Portugal with a per capita GNP lower than Mexico, Uruguay, Puerto Rico, Trinidad and Tobago or Venezuela (and Greece with one less than the last two countries mentioned) may strongly object to increase aid in that direction. (See Table 3)

On the other hand, it is not secret to anyone that Spain is going to push hard for a change in the geographic distribution of EC cooperation aid toward Latin America. Most of the foreign aid offered by Spain is directed towards Latin American countries (e.g. 69% of the total for the period 1969-1973). But the aid effort is reduced, representing only 0,07% of GNP (in 1980), about five times less than the effort done by an average OECD country. This is why, one may think that as long as Spain itself does not give the example and rases considerably its bilateral aid levels there is no chance that the EC would follow her in her aspirations. In that respect, Spain's active or passive participation in, or cooperation with some Latin American institutions (e.g. ECLA, Andean Group, SELA, Inter-American Development Bank) may not be of much help. On the other hand, Spanish pressure may prevent the future suppression of some Latin American NICs from the list of beneficiaries of the EC's GSP scheme.[17]

Spain's Policies towards Latin American-EC Relations after the Enlargement

Spain has been striving during the long negotiations for accession into the EC to obtain the same treatment for Latin America that the ACP countries are getting. This has proved to be an impossible mission for many reasons. Only a Joint Declaration of Intent and a unilateral declaration by Spain was attached to the Accession Treaty. Backing by Latin American countries has not been forthcoming; many of those countries are considered to be NICs by the Ten and therefore should deserve in their eyes a different treatment than ACP countries. This is not to speak of different foreign policy perceptions of Spain in relations to the non-Latin members of the EC. In this respect and as Berrocal (1980) stresses, the Mediterranean dimension of the Enlargement takes priority over Latin American problems, not because of the severity of its

Table 3. Per capita GNP

Spain	4800
Greece	3970
Portugal	2190
Trinidad and Tobago	6900
Venezuela	4100
Puerto Rico	2890
Uruguay	2490
Mexico	2240
Argentina	2030
Chile	1870

Source: World Bank Atlas 1985

impact on the Mediterranean Basin, but because proximity and other highly strategic factors, all absent in the case of the American continent. Incidentally, this is also true for Greece and Spain themselves; in spite of the fact that culturally speaking Latin America may be closer to Spain than, say, Turkey. In other words, the pocket and the gun are not located where the heart lies.[18] And paradoxically, one of the countries that seems to be going to be hurt on various fronts by the Enlargement, namely Brazil, is not Spanish-speaking. Together with Argentina, Uruguay and Colombia, these are the countries that should be most concerned by the Enlargement. Since all of them are NICs, Spain could realistically try to persuade its partners in the Community to conclude bilateral agreements, using as a model some of the most developed EC-Mediterranean agreements (e.g. with Malta, Turkey or Israel) rather than the ACP framework. Such a solution based on partial reciprocity would go a long way in the direction of the reduction in trade dependence from the US, so much desired by Latin Americans. Quite another matter would be to convince them that two-way free trade is good for them too.....

Notes

1. But note that for many agricultural products and commodities of interest to Latin America, the Common Customs Tariff duties apply from March 1, 1986, with the exception of cocoa beans and coffee for which the deadline is January 1, 1991.
2. Protocols are to be negotiated fixing the exact way of application of the "acquis communautaire".
3. See note 2 above.
4. See note 2 above.
5. Greece actually did withdraw in June 1980, as required by the Accession Treaty.
6. See, e.g., the contributions of Guzman, Beihardt, Oldekap and Berrocal in Institut d'Etudes Européennes (1981); see also Granda Alva et al. 1984).
7. The same holds true for trade between Portugal and EFTA, of which Portugal was an original member.
8. See Riera (1985).
9. In relation to line 8 the assumption is that the few concessions relating to agricultural imports that the EC has been giving under the GSP scheme cannot compare with the quite or very favourable treatment which respectively Mediterranean or ACP countries have received.
10. See note 6 above; Sebastian (1985) reports on other Latin American empirical studies, none of which refers to many of the effects expected by this author.
11. Amazingly enough, nobody seems to bother asking compensation from EFTA countries for the erosion in preferential treatment received under the different GSP schemes.
12. In UNCTAD's jargon, one would speak of "preference erosion".
13. Sampson and Snape (1980) show how the present variable levy-export restitution

184

system has lowered world wheat and barley prices by a factor of 3% to 11% in relation to those which have been in force in 1976 without the system.

14. And more directly still, for those products not covered by the Community's GSP scheme, the alignment of the Three's tariffs toward the CCT implies a reduction in protection levels, trade creation must be by definition the outcome.

15. See the excellent study by J. Donges (1979) *Towards Spain's Accession into the EEC*, Kiel, Kiel Working Paper nr. 94, for a discussion on unexploited economies of scale.

16. Moreover, access to European Investment Bank funds to institute structural change of technological improvement may stimulate further investment by private sources.

17. See Weston A. et al. (1980), pp. 165-76 on graduation, differentiation and conditionality in the aplication of GSP benefits. Interestingly, Venezuela, Argentina, Uruguay, Brazil and Mexico are all mentioned as possible candidates (others would say victims) linked to these innovations.

18. In this respect, this author together with many others dismisses outright the naive "theory", which asserts that Spain is going to be a "bridge" between Europe and Latin America. As de Sebastian (1985) says, neither of the two blocks are in need of a mediator. See, also, Institut d'Etudes Européennes (1981), p. 30.

References

Baklanoff, E. (1985), Spain's Emergence as a Middle Idustrial Power. The Basis and Structure of Spanish-Latin American Economic Interrelations, *AEI Occasional Papers*, Nr. 11, April.

Berrocal, L. (1980), El Dialogo Euro-Latinoamericano: Mas allá de un Neocolo nialismo larvado?, *Revista de Instituciones Europeas*, vol. 7, nr.3, September-December, pp.947-67.

Bodemer, K. (1985), Perspectivas de las relaciones interregionales entre la Comunidad Europea y America Latina, *Integración Latinoamericana*, April, pp.22-31.

Commission of the European Communities (1983), *The European Community and Latin America*, Europe Information, nr 68/83, June.

Commission of the European Communities (1984), *Accords et autres engagements bilateraux qui lient les Communautés a des pays tiers*, Brussels, January.

Council of the European Communities (1985), *Instruments concerning the Accession of the Kingdom of Spain and the Portuguese Republic to the European Communities*, Vols I, II, III.

Eckstein, A.M. (1985), "Retrouvailles" timides entre les "presque douze" et l'Amérique Latine, *Revue du Marché Commun*, nr.286, April, pp.197-99.

El Pais, June 12 1985.

Eurostat (1985), *Analysis of EC-Latin America Trade*, Luxembourg, Office des publications officielles des Communautés européennes.

Granda Alva, G. and Garcia, J.L. (1984), La Cooperatión para el Desarrollo de las Comunidades Europeas y sus relaciones con America Latina: Un reto para España, *Estudios Internacionales*, vol. 5, nr.3, April-June, pp.443-58.

Institut d'Etudes Européenes (1981), *La Communauté Européenne et l'Amérique Latine*, Brussels, Editions de l'Université de Bruxelles.

Riera, L. (1985), *España, pais comunitario: El desarme arancelario*, Barcelona, ESADE.

Sampson, G. and Snape, R. (1980), Effects of the EEC's Variable Import Levies, *Journal of Political Economy*, vol 88, nr.5, October, pp.1026-40.

Sampson, G. and Yeats, A. (1977), An Evaluation of the Common Agricultural Policy as a Barrier Facing Agricultural Exports to the European Community, *American Journal of Agricultural Economics*, February, pp.99-106.

Sebastian, L. de (1985), España, es realmente puente entre Europe y America Latina, unpublished paper, June.

Weston, A. et al. (1980), *The EEC's Generalised System of Preferences*, London, Overseas Development Institute.

Index